T0275103

The Rise and Fall of the

Freedman's Savings Bank

and its Lasting Socio-Economic Impact
on Black America

By Rodney A. Brooks

First published March 2024
by
Spiramus Press Ltd
102 Blandford Street
London W1U 8AG

www.spiramus.com

ISBN
9781910151495 Paperback
9781913507527 Digital

Front Cover Image: "Office of the Freedmen's Bureau, Memphis, Tennessee" from The New York Public Library
Page viii image: Thomas Nast, "Waiting", Published in Harper's Weekly, 1879

Table of Contents

Table of Contents

Acknowledgements

There are a few people whose help made this book possible. Thanks to Hollis Gentry Brown, at the National Museum of African American History and Culture, who guided me through the troves of information at the National Archives. I would also like to thank research assistant Mollie Jackson, my former colleague from USA TODAY, and Rep. Kweisi Mfume, who found the time in his busy schedule to share his knowledge about the bank, and who is a fellow history buff who can cite facts about events 150 years ago right off the top of his head.

And a very special thank you to my wife and life partner, Dr. Sheila Brooks, entrepreneur, author and educator, who has provided both inspiration and support throughout our 35-year union.

"Hold fast to dreams, for if dreams die, life is a broken-winged bird that cannot fly."

Langston Hughes

"It was obvious that people who were in slavery were not ignorant. Du Bois says there were 27 Black millionaires in Louisiana at the time of emancipation. There were tradesmen and craftsmen who had done all kinds of things. But they understood that in addition to the right to vote, to be free, you had to have access to capital."

Andrew Young

"50 years after the Freedman's Bank"

Preface

My father, William Francis Brooks, died at 43 years old, when I was just 16 and a sophomore in high school. His early and unexpected death left many holes in my life, among them my family history.

Like my father, I was born in Baltimore, but my family left when I was five years old. Most of my family – both my father's and my mother's families – still lived in Baltimore when we moved to Newark, New Jersey.

I am forever grateful that my parents piled their five kids into the family station wagon every summer for the 3½ hours trek south to Baltimore so we would grow up knowing both sides of our family.

I was also very fortunate. I got to meet both grandparents on my father's side and my grandfather and step-grandmother on my mother's side. My parents left us to stay each summer with our grandparents, aunts and uncles in Baltimore or Philadelphia. I'm sure it gave them a break from raising five kids, but it also gave us an opportunity to get to know and to bond with our extended family.

We were much too young even to think about the stories our grandparents could tell. It was much later in life that I felt the need to know my family.

It wasn't until years later that I was able to discover my family's history – my personal Black history. I was able to trace both my father's and mother's family histories back to slavery, and beyond.

That brings us to the Freedman's Savings Bank. Many Americans are probably familiar with the Freedmen's Bureau, created after the Civil War to help the newly freed slaves survive and assimilate into the American society. But few are aware of the history of the Freedman's Bank, which was created as an entirely separate entity, to give Black Civil War veterans a place to save and grow their money.

But it has provided another way for Black families to find information about their descendent, especially those who are related to the Black soldiers who fought for the Union during the Civil War.

To me it was amazing that BBC reporter Szu Ping Chan, traveled all the way across the pond to do a special radio report on the Freedman's Bank. Just as fascinating, she was able to track down descendants of some of the original depositors, some who knew little or nothing about their family histories or the bank.

So it was with great enthusiasm that I undertook the effort of telling the history of a little-known "quasi-Black" bank that was born with great hope and died less than ten years later, a killer of Black dreams.

Many historians and economists say the unfortunate closing of the Freedman's Savings Bank still impacts the culture and history of Black people in the United States, and not in a good way.

Personally, I traced my family's roots to a little town in rural Maryland where my paternal family had been enslaved. From there, I tracked my heritage back to Nigeria, where my ninth great grandfather was born in 1650. It was difficult, and it was time consuming. But it was well worth it when I hit pay dirt. National Geographic featured that story only in June 2023.

I put that same enthusiasm into my research into the Freedman's Bank. I hope my research makes it easier for people, Black and white, to look back on a particularly tumultuous time for all Black Americans – the post-Civil War period and Reconstruction. It was a time that should have been filled with hopes and dreams and instead was filled with fear and violence.

Out of that turmoil grew something that was good, a bank that was open for business for Black folks, something that had not previously existed in this country. To tell you how big a deal that was, the poor Blacks who opened accounts at the branches in the South used to dress up for their visits.

It also tells you how important the creation of the bank was when you consider that the first truly Black-owned bank did not open until the late 1880s by a former slave.

Black History Month is celebrated every February in the US and Canada (and every October in Ireland and the UK). But every day we can learn about something or someone we didn't know about in Black history.

Ask my long-time friend Carl Mack, an engineer by training and self-taught walking Black history encyclopedia, who created a 365-day Black history calendar that features a story of a Black person every day of the year, many of whom you may not have heard of. Carl has also created a new calendar that celebrates the lives of an outstanding Black women, past and present.

Ask my eldest son, R. Alan Brooks, who created displays and accompanying graphic novels featuring Black history at both the Denver Art Museum and at the Denver Museum of Contemporary Art – stories about mostly forgotten people and places from the American West.

Ask my wife, Dr. Sheila Brooks, who has written about trailblazing Black women newspaper editors and publishers who fought for equality for Blacks and women and who often had to run for their lives. While many know about Ida B. Wells-Barnett, fewer know names like Mary Ann Shad Curry or Lucile Bluford.

Ask me. We are still making history. I was the first in my family to go to college. I was the first Black reporter at my first job out of college. Later I was the first Black editor and the first business editor of any color at my second newspaper job. After a 40-plus year career in newspaper journalism, today I am in the National Association of Black Journalists Hall of Fame.

There is so much Black history in America and in the world. But there is also so much Black history that we still haven't learned.

I took great pleasure in taking a deep dive into the history of the Freedman's Savings & Trust Company. Each day's research led me to learn something new about both Black history and American history.

And even though the bank failed 150 years ago, Black America is still feeling the effects in so many different ways – mostly through American's persistent racial wealth gap.

I'm happy to share the story of the Freedman's Bank and its everlasting impact on Blacks in America with my children, my grandchildren and with you.

Rodney A. Brooks

Introduction

Black history is under siege in cities, counties and states across America. Efforts to whitewash or deny the teaching of Black history and remove books authored by Black authors from public and school libraries are gaining momentum.

But, like the Jim Crow laws that legally imposed segregation on Black America, these efforts have resulted in a resolve and determination to find alternative methods to ensure that *all* children receive a full and proper education.

Still, efforts to deny Black history are proving to be both damaging and divisive. Stressed librarians and teachers are quitting. White Americans, especially children, will be prevented from knowing, understanding and acknowledging the history of Black people in America – from the horrors of slavery and the Jim Crow South to the shining light that came with the ascent of President Barack Obama into the White House.

That's unfortunate, especially when you consider that "blacks lived in a different time and a different reality in this country," according to journalist and historian Lerone Bennett Jr. in his book *The Challenge of Blackness*.

The American Civil Liberties Union (ACLU) says that state legislatures in more than 30 states have introduced bills to limit the discussion of racial history – prompted by the emergence of critical race theory as a subject of political fearmongering in white America. More than 300 books by predominantly Black authors discussing race, gender, and sexuality, have been banned in the last year alone.

Journalist Nikole Hannah-Jones, creator of the award-winning New York Times' *1619 Project*, discussed the backlash in the book that was born from a project by the staff of *The New York Times* and *The New York Times Magazine* on the 400th anniversary of the start slavery. This was a Herculean effort that focused on the consequences of slavery in the history of the United States, also called *The 1619 Project*. The book *1619 Project* is on many of those banned book lists mentioned above.

> "As the reach of the 1619 Project grew, so did the backlash. A small group of historians publicly attempted to discredit the project by challenging its historical interpretations and pointing to what they said were historical errors. They did not agree with our framing, which treated slavery and anti-Blackness as foundational to America. They did not like our assertion that Black Americans have served as this nation's most ardent freedom fighters and have waged their battles mostly alone, or the idea that so much of modern American life has been shaped not by the majestic ideals of our founding but by its grave hypocrisy."[1]

Hannah-Jones got a much more personal look at that backlash when she was offered a tenured faculty position in the School of Journalism at the University of North Carolina. The offer was rescinded after criticism of her role in *The 1619 Project* from white conservatives. After protests both within the university and across the nation, the tenure offer was restored. Hannah-Jones rejected it and instead joined the faculty of the historically Black Howard University in Washington, D.C.

Meanwhile, Texas A&M reached a $1 million settlement with a Black journalism professor after her appointment was rescinded because of white conservative backlash over of her work on diversity, equity and inclusion.

We have come full circle. Black history had been denied and ignored in white America for centuries. But first the Harlem Renaissance and then the 1970s saw a surge in interest in Black culture and Black history, especially in inner cities and on college campuses. What began as Negro History Week in 1926 with Carter G. Woodson became Black History Month, which was originated by Black educators and students at Kent State University in 1970.

There was another resurgence in interest in Black history during the social justice protests of 2020 following the murders of George Floyd and other unarmed Black American men and women at the hands of police. Many Americans for the first time learned about stories like the 1921 Tulsa massacre, in which white mobs burned down a vibrant and thriving Black community in Tulsa, Oklahoma (homes, businesses and churches) and murdered innocent men, women and children.

And Americans, Black and white, began celebrating Juneteenth, when the last of the enslaved Blacks were emancipated, in Texas in 1865, as a federal holiday in 2021. The holiday had a long tradition and history of celebrations in some Black communities, in the U.S. especially in Texas.

Black history celebrates outstanding achievements by Black men, women and culture from the first day the African slaves set foot in Virginia. But it is also filled with atrocities, pain and despair, such as the horrors of centuries of slavery, lynchings, race riots, Jim Crow and institutional racism.

Perhaps nothing captures those mixed emotions like the history of the Freedman's Savings & Trust Co. Established in 1865 by President Abraham Lincoln and the U.S. Congress at the same time they created with the much better-known Freedmen's Bureau, which was tasked with providing social, educational and financial assistance to the hundreds of thousands of newly freed slaves.

Introduction

The Freedman's Savings Bank was established primarily to give Black Civil War soldiers and veterans – flush with cash wages and bounties – access to a bank to save and grow their money, something that was denied at white banking institutions. The Black soldiers, many of them former slaves who had never earned money of their own, also needed a way to send much-needed cash to their families.

The bank also offered Blacks, both former slaves and freedmen, the opportunity to learn lessons about finances and money and training in banking jobs that were not available at white banking institutions.

One appeal was that the newly freed Blacks believed the Freedman's Bank was backed by the government – misled by the advertising and promotion. It was not backed by the government, as they disappointedly discovered later. The bank also had prominent promotors, including Black leaders like Frederick Douglass, Civil War generals and Northern white abolitionists.

There was initial success. The bank grew quickly to 37 branches in 17 states, mostly in the South and Southwest, but also in major cities in the Northeast like New York, Washington, D.C. and Philadelphia. That expansive branch system was unprecedented at that time, even for large white banking institutions, and actually led to many of the bank's problems.

The Freedman's Savings Bank grew much too fast, and eventually the early success was overtaken by incompetence, a world economic downturn and rampant corruption by the all-white male leaders of the institution.

Douglass was brought in as president of the bank to help revive the troubled institution and invested $10,000 of his own money to help restore confidence in the bank. But by then it was too late.

Once he saw the bank's books, he realized that the situation was hopeless. The bank foundered, and then collapsed. And in 1874 Congress moved to shut it down – and with it went the hopes, dreams and savings of thousands of Blacks.

The closing of the Freedman's Bank did much more than shatter the dreams of former slaves and freedmen – including Douglass. It left 61,144 depositors with losses of nearly $3 million (more than $80 million today). After years of waiting, some depositors recouped only a portion of their money. Most of the poorest received nothing.

Joseph Haskins, founder and retired CEO of Harbor Bank, a Black-owned commercial bank in Baltimore, Maryland commented:

> "The Freedmen's bank for me has both positive and negative sort of reactions. It is positive in the sense of it providing an avenue that didn't exist previously for African Americans to be able to deposit and create savings… And the negative is that it was put into a perilous posture by opportunistic whites who used those dollars inappropriately and leaving the bank in a precarious position."

It was a sad and devastating end to something that started out with so much hope and promise.

Today economists and historians point to the failure of the Freedman's Savings Bank as a contributor to this nation's racial wealth gap, which remains significant and continues to grow. The median wealth of white American families is nearly seven times that of Black families.

So, we're only left to imagine the possibilities – if those millions lost by Blacks depositors when the Freedman's Bank shut down 150 years ago had been used back then to buy farms, homes and property, and to educate their children and grandchildren – and what those resources would have meant for Black generational wealth.

That's not to say there would not be a racial wealth gap in the United States had the Freedman's Bank survived. But most of us agree that the impact on Black Americans at the time was both devastating and long-lasting.

Constantine Yannelis, associate professor of finance at The University of Chicago Booth School of Business and faculty research fellow at the National Bureau of Economic Research said:

"I think a lot of the disparities we see today have their roots in that period, in the aftermath of the Civil War, Reconstruction and the period before."

These economic disparities are very real and rooted in American history. And no discussion of the racial wealth gap would be complete unless we first have a thorough look back at the history of the sometimes-violent racism and discrimination that Blacks have endured in America going back even before the birth of the United States.

Chapter 1: A bank failure 150 years ago still haunts Black America today

The numbers tell a story of a dismal economic reality permeated by a history of brutal and pervasive racism and discrimination. The Black-white racial wealth gap in America is enormous and continues to grow. The median wealth of Black families is $24,100 compared to median white family's wealth which averages $165,000.

Prosperity Now, a Washington, D.C. organization that promotes economic equality, predicts that the median wealth of Black families will drop to zero by 2053.[2]

When we look back on the causes of that racial wealth gap, one, in particular, started out as a positive way to help the newly freed slaves and Black Civil War soldiers achieve financial freedom and independence. It certainly didn't end that up way.

British journalist Szu Ping Chan said in her 2023 BBC radio documentary:

> "This is the story of the Freedman's Bank. Established by the U.S. Government in 1865 after the end of slavery and the Civil War, it failed nine years later. You may not even have heard of the Freedman's Bank, but this little-known episode in Black history destroyed the savings of thousands of families and left a legacy of distrust that is still felt to this day."

In her Ph.D. dissertation, *"Intergenerational Effects of Wealth Loss Evidence from The Freedman's Bank,"* UCLA student Xuanyu (Iris) Fu, studied whether a parental wealth shock stemming from the failure of the Freedman's Bank had an effect on the educational outcomes of the children of bank depositors. Her research found that children from families who lost a higher proportion of their wealth when the bank closed were less likely to attend school after the bank's failure.

The bank was brought down by much of the same greed, corruption and discrimination that has stifled Black American progress since the first slaves landed on the shores of what is now the Virginia in United States in 1619. Looking back in history, it was one of many historical events that led to the destruction of Black generational wealth and the ever-widening racial wealth gap.

The institution of slavery

Between 1501 and 1867 nearly 13 million African people were kidnapped, forced onto European and American ships and trafficked across the Atlantic Ocean where they were enslaved, abused, and forever separated from their homes, families, and cultures. An estimated 1.8 million, or nearly 14.5 percent, did not survive the voyage, or Middle Passage[1], as it was called. The death rate of the Middle Passage had been as high as 30 percent in the early days of the slave trade in the 16th Century.

After centuries of enslavement in the U.S., the descendants of these Black men, women and children were released into a hostile and deeply racist American South with virtually nothing. Thousands died from starvation, disease and exposure. After the death by assassination of President Abraham Lincoln, programs that were enacted by Congress to help the formerly enslaved were discontinued or ignored.

---

[1] The Middle Passage was a leg of the triangular route of the slave ships, which left Europe with guns, ammunition, cotton cloth, etc., to trade for slaves in Africa, then, to the Americas and West Indies to trade the slaves for rum, cotton and sugar from plantations. They then sailed back to Europe with those raw materials

Repeated attempts at slavery reparations have been met with unrelenting opposition from white Americans, especially hostile Republican-led state legislatures and Congress. William A. Darity Jr. and A. Kirsten Mullen, co-authors of the book *From Here to Equality, Reparations for Black Americans in the Twenty-First Century*, estimated that the U.S. government should pay $14 trillion in reparations to Black Americans for slavery and legal segregation.

A racist U.S. president sabotaged Reconstruction

The Freedmen's Bureau was created in 1865 during the Lincoln administration, by an act of Congress to aid former slaves through food and housing, oversight, education, health care, and employment contracts with private landowners. After Lincoln's assassination in 1865, a follow-up Freedmen's Bureau Bill was vetoed by his vice president and successor, President Andrew Johnson.

Johnson, a former slaveowner, fought to sabotage and dismantle The Freedmen's Bureau and halt Reconstruction. He believed that Blacks were incapable of managing their own lives and did not deserve to vote, even telling a group of Black White House visitors that they should go to another country. He gave amnesty and pardons to former Confederates and returned their property, except their slaves. The Freedmen's Bureau was eventually disbanded during the first term of President Ulysses S. Grant.[3]

> "Between 1865 and 1876 thousands of Black women, men and children were killed, attacked, sexually assaulted and terrorized by white mobs and individuals who were shielded from arrest and prosecution. White perpetrators of lawless, random violence against formerly enslaved people were almost never held accountable – instead, they were frequently celebrated. Emboldened Confederate veterans and former enslavers organized a reign of terror that effectively nullified constitutional amendments designed to

provide Black people equal protection and the right to vote."[4]

Activist and Civil Rights leader W.E.B. Du Bois later wrote in *Black Reconstruction in America*, "The slave went free, stood a brief moment in the sun, then moved back again toward slavery."[5]

The collapse of Freedman's Savings Bank

Often overlooked in the racial wealth gap is a key event in the years following the abolition of slavery in the United States. The Freedman's Savings and Trust Company was established by Congress in 1865.

Thousands flocked to the branches that went up, mostly in the Southern states, but also in big cities like New York, Philadelphia and Washington, D.C. The bank grew fast – perhaps too fast. It grew to 37 branches – an achievement that even white-owned banks had not achieved at this time. But with that unprecedented branch system came problems that would ultimately lead to disaster.

Communication between the bank's leaders in the palatial Washington, D.C. headquarters and the far-reaching branches could take days or weeks. Oversight was virtually non-existent, especially considering there was only one bank auditor to serve the entire system.

The bank became a depository for the soldiers' bounty payments, and later, their pensions. But later depositors included all kinds of Black Americans – freedmen and women, Black businesses, Black churches and civic and social organizations. They also included Black children. Unsurprisingly, most of the deposits were small – many Blacks were receiving money and wages for the first time in their lives.

They thought they were putting their money in a "Black bank," though that was not really the case. They were also led to believe that their money was safe, protected by the United States government. But the bank failed nine years later, in 1874, wiping out the savings (and the dreams) of thousands of Blacks, failing in its mission to offer financial education and destroying generational wealth for years to come.

The concept was commendable. But incompetence, theft, a worldwide financial crisis and corruption at all levels contributed to the bank's demise.

> "Unfortunately, fraud and embezzlement at the hands of the bank's majority-white upper management and board of trustees, coupled with the Panic of 1873, led to the bank's closure, leaving more than 61,144 depositors unable to retrieve accounts valued at $2,993,790.68.[6]

> "An idea that began as a well-meaning experiment in philanthropy had turned into an economic nightmare for tens of thousands African Americans who had entrusted their hard-earned money to the bank," says *The Freedman's Savings and Trust Company and African American Genealogical Research.*

> "Perhaps more far-reaching than the immediate loss of their tiny deposits, was the deadening effect the bank's closure had on many of the depositors' hopes and dreams for a brighter future. The bank's demise left bitter feelings of betrayal, abandonment, and distrust of the American banking system that would remain in the African American community for many years."[7]

In addition, many historians and economists have said the failure of the bank had long term implications for Black Americans.

The late journalist and historian Lerone Bennett, Jr., former senior editor of *Ebony Magazine* wrote in his classic book, *The Shaping of Black America:*

> "The failure of the Freedman's Bank had repercussions of the gravest sort in the Black community. The newly freed Blacks lost more than one million of their hard-bought dollars, and the government made no effort to reimburse them. The loss in the realm of the spirit was equally great."[8]

But just as damaging was that the resulting distrust of banks and financial institutions among Black Americans would last for years.

U.S. Rep. Kweisi Mfume, a former president and CEO of the NAACP says that even though there was not a great deal of news reporting at that time, news travelled through the Black community through word of mouth. That resulted in a distrust of banks, and repercussions are still being felt today.

Booker T. Washington, the prominent Black civil rights leader of the late 1800s and founder of Tuskegee Institute (now Tuskegee University), who was born into slavery, wrote:

> "When they found out that they had lost, or been swindled out of their savings, they lost faith in savings banks, and it was a long time after this before it was possible to mention a savings bank for Negroes without some reference being made to the disaster of (the Freedman's Bank)."

40 acres and a mule

The federal government promised 40 acres and a mule to the formerly enslaved multiple times after the Civil War. It turned out to be an empty promise. After President Lincoln was assassinated, Johnson dismantled the program.

Gary Cunningham, former CEO of Prosperity Now, said if Black people had received their 40 acres in a mule America would not have the economic inequalities that we have today.

Meanwhile, 1.5 million white settlers were given 160-acre land grants. According to William A. Darity, Samuel DuBois Cook Distinguished Professor of Public Policy at the Duke University Sanford School of Public Policy, this was more impactful than the collapse of the Freedman's Bank in contributing to the racial wealth gap.

Darity says that there were four million Freedmen in 1865, each of whom should have received 10 acres of land. If the average price of one acre of land was $10 back then, then the total value of the land due to the Freedmen was $400 million or $100 per person. Compounded at 4 percent interest, the present value of the total will be about $196 billion or about $50,000 per person, he says.

Political commentator Roland Martin, CEO of Blackstar Network and host of *"Roland Martin Unfiltered"* said:

> "Because of the failure of America to provide that 40 acres and a mule as soon as people of African descent come out of slavery, we are completely behind… From that point, in 1863 onwards, we (Black Americans) are operating at a deficit in everything – housing, jobs, health care, and education. We're in a constant state of trying to catch up."

Racial violence and the destruction of vibrant Black communities

Violent white mobs destroyed vibrant Black communities in Tulsa, Oklahoma and dozens of other American cities, including in Philadelphia, Atlanta, Houston, Rosewood, New York and Charleston, South Carolina. Armed whites also overthrew an elected Black government in Wilmington, North Carolina in 1896.

Consultant and politician Maya Rockeymoore Cummings commented:

> "Through a series of actions like lynchings and random killings, etc., basically to keep Black people from finding their rights or from getting ahead of themselves, (whites) actively sought to basically destroy black wealth... Because any Black wealth that exists, was a direct threat to not only the system of white supremacy, but the psychology of white supremacy."

The Equal Justice Initiative, a private non-profit organization dedicated to criminal justice reform based in Montgomery, Alabama, says it has documented at least 12 large scale massacres in Louisiana, Alabama, Texas, Tennessee, Mississippi, and South Carolina between 1872 and 1876. Many targeted politically active African Americans.

In Tulsa alone 1,256 homes were burned, 200 others were looted. Two newspapers, a school, a library, a hospital, churches, hotels, stores and other Black-owned businesses were among the buildings destroyed or damaged by fire.

The Oklahoma Commission formed in 1997 to investigate the riot concluded that the total property damage was approximately $1.8 million. If 1,200 median priced houses in Tulsa were destroyed today, the loss would be around $150 million. The additional loss of other assets, including cash, personal belongings, and commercial property, might bring the total to over $200 million.[9]

The Second Amendment of the Bill of Rights granted citizens of the new country the right to bear arms. But the enslaved were not considered citizens, and in most states, even free Black people were kept from exercising their legal rights. Though it did not explicitly say so, the Second Amendment was motivated in large part by a need for the new federal government to assure whites in the South that they would be able to defend themselves against 39Black people.[10]

Redlining and housing discrimination

In the 1930s the federal government, banks and other lenders created city maps to determine where they would lend money to people buying homes. Black inner-city neighborhoods were outlined in red. Banks refused to lend money to buy or even improve homes in those areas. Researchers at the National Community Reinvestment Coalition, the University of Wisconsin-Milwaukee and the University of Richmond found that "the history of redlining, segregation and the disinvestment reduced Black wealth, but also impacted health and longevity" of Blacks.

As the United States Commission on Civil Rights said in its 1959 report:

> "Some of the effects of the housing inequalities of minorities can be seen with the eye, some can be shown by statistics, some can only be measured in the mind and heart."

The U.S. Department of Agriculture's racism devastated Black farmers

Black farmers were systematically denied assistance from the U.S. Department of Agriculture, which also played a major role in bankrupting Black farmers. A National Public Radio (NPR) analysis of USDA data found that Black farmers received a disproportionately low share of direct loans, causing many to lose their land to foreclosure.

Black farmers won a $1.2 billion discrimination settlement from the USDA in 2010. But NPR says thousands of Black farmers lost out because of confusing paperwork and filing deadlines. By then the number of active Black farmers had dwindled from 14 percent of the U.S. total to 1.4 percent.

Black World War II veterans were denied the benefits of the GI Bill

The wide disparity in the implementation of the GI Bill was a major driver in the wealth, income and education gaps between Black and white veterans. The language in the bill didn't exclude Black veterans, but racist white Southern politicians did everything they could do to ensure that Black veterans did not benefit.

Also, the developers of Levittown planned communities in several states offered the dream of affordable home ownership to returning World War II veterans, but refused to sell to Black veterans, and in fact, wrote discriminatory racial covenants into each deed.

Considering that housing wealth is about half of total household wealth, Black veterans and their descendants were denied access to what is probably today billions in generational household wealth.

Racism in education

The education of Blacks was actually illegal in some states. Some of those who violated those laws were prosecuted and jailed. According to the 1847 Virginia Criminal Code:

> "Any white person who shall assemble with slaves, [or] free negroes . . . for the purpose of instructing them to read or write, . . . shall be punished by confinement in the jail . . . and by fine . . ."

Under this code, Margaret Douglass, of Norfolk, Virginia, was arrested, imprisoned, and fined when authorities discovered that she was teaching "free colored children" of the Christ's Church Sunday school to read and write.

Courts at the state and federal levels upheld racial segregation multiple times before *Brown vs. the Board of Education* outlawed it in 1954. When a federal judge ordered schools in Prince Edward County, Virginia to integrate, the county shut down the entire school system instead, offering tuition grants to support schools for white students. Black children were shut out of the county's public schools for five years before the courts intervened.

W.E.B. Du Bois wrote in *The Souls of Black Folk:*

> "The South believed an educated Negro to be a dangerous Negro... And the South was not wholly wrong; for education among all kinds of men always has had, and always will have, an element of danger and revolution, of dissatisfaction and discontent. Nevertheless, men strive to know."[11]

Racism in health care and the infamous Tuskegee syphilis experiment

The U.S. healthcare system practiced systematic discrimination against Blacks for centuries.

An effort to provide at least some hospital care for Blacks prompted the establishment of the earliest segregated black hospitals. Georgia Infirmary, established in Savannah in 1832, was the first such facility. By the end of the nineteenth century, several others had been founded, including Raleigh, North Carolina's St. Agnes Hospital in 1896 and Atlanta's MacVicar Infirmary in 1900.[12] Later Black hospitals were mostly available to Blacks who lived in large urban centers like Washington, D.C., New York and Chicago.

Before the passage of Medicare and Medicaid, the U.S. healthcare system was segregated. Segregated hospitals in the South complied with Jim Crow laws and excluded Blacks from white-only hospitals or provided accommodations for Blacks in the basements. When Medicare threatened to withhold federal funding from hospitals that practiced racial discrimination under the Civil Rights Act of 1964, hospitals desegregated almost overnight.

But nothing captured the overt racism in the U.S. like the Tuskegee experiment, conducted by the U.S. Public Health Service and the Centers for Disease Control and Tuskegee Institute from 1932 to 1972. Four hundred Black men were promised free medical care and thought they were being treated for syphilis but were unknowingly part of a study on the effects of the disease if left untreated. More than one hundred died.

The revelation of that experiment led to a distrust of health care and government agencies that is still prevalent among Black Americans today. Health experts and community leaders said it was part of the reason for the resistance among Blacks to get COVID-19 vaccines during the world pandemic.

Jim Crow and legal segregation

Jim Crow laws were both local and state laws, mostly the Southern states, in the late 19th and 20th Centuries that enforced racial segregation. They remained in force until 1965. One goal was to reverse political and economic gains made by Southern Blacks during reconstruction. The laws mandated segregation at public facilities in the former Confederate states.

Blair Condoll, a political science professor at Dillard University in New Orleans, said in an interview with Voice of America:

> "There are still effects between Jim Crow and slavery before it. That's hundreds of years of this society having two tiers – one for white Americans and another for Black. We can't just erase that in a generation or two."

Slavery, Jim Crow segregation and The Freedman's Bank

All these events over centuries in American history played some part in the situation that Blacks find themselves in today. With this narrative our focus will be on the impact of the Freedman's Bank. But we will also see just how interrelated these racial shocks are and how together they have destroyed the hopes and dreams of millions Black Americans.

And, we will see just how damaging the failure of the Freedman's Bank was to Blacks, and why we are still feeling the impact 150 years later.

Chapter 2: A brief history of slavery in the United States

The so called "peculiar institution" of slavery is one of the most horrific and violent episodes in the history of the world. Two million Black Africans perished in the infamous Middle Passage. They arrived in the Americas to a legacy of pain, repression and generational bondage. They were demoralized and dehumanized. All vestiges of their religion, education and culture were legally banned. Families were split up, sold and separated. And they were freed centuries later into a system of legalized discrimination, violence and destitution.

Between 1501 and 1867 nearly 13 million African people were kidnapped, forced onto European and American ships and trafficked across the Atlantic Ocean to be enslaved, abused, and forever separated from their homes, families, ancestors and cultures.[13]

The slave ship *San Juan Bautista* departed Luanda, Angola with 350 enslaved captives from Ndongo in West Central Africa. Its destination was Vera Cruz, Mexico, but it was attacked by English privateer ships *White Lion* and *Treasurer*. The English ships stole around 60 of the surviving Africans and sailed for Virginia.

Many trace the true start of racial human in bondage in what is now the United States back to 1619, when approximately 30 enslaved Africans landed at Point Comfort in Hampton, Virginia on the *White Lion*. The *Treasurer* arrived a few days later with more slaves. They were sold to Virginia Company officials in exchange for supplies – the first recorded Africans to arrive in England's mainland American colonies.

Journalist Nikole Hannah-Jones wrote in *The 1619 Project*:

"In late August 1619 a ship arrived in the British colony of Virginia bearing a cargo of somewhere between twenty and thirty enslaved people from Africa… Their arrival led to the barbaric and unprecedented system of American chattel slavery that would last for the next 250 years. This is sometimes referred to as our country's original sin, but it is more than just that: It is the source of so much that still defines the United States."[14]

Although English colonists in Virginia did not invent slavery, and the transition from a handful of bound African laborers to a legalized system of full-blown chattel slavery took many decades, 1619 marks the beginning of race-based bondage that defined the African American experience.[15]

The late Lerone Bennett Jr., an *Ebony Magazine* editor and historian, wrote:

"It was… August, 344 years before the March on Washington, 346 years before Watts, and 212 years before Nat Turner's war, that 'a Dutch man of War' sailed up the river James and landed the first generation of black Americans at Jamestown, Virginia.

No one knows the hour or the day of the black landing. But there is not the slightest doubt about the month.

The ship that sailed up the James on a day we will never know was the beginning of America…That ship brought the black gold that made capitalism possible in America; it brought slave-built Monticello and slave-built Mount Vernon and the Cotton Kingdom and the graves on the slopes of Gettysburg."[16]

It took only a few decades after the arrival of first enslaved Africans in Virginia before white settlers in America demanded a new world defined by a racial caste system. The 1664 General Assembly of Maryland decreed that all Negroes shall serve *durante vita*, hard labor "for life." This enslavement would be sustained by the threat of brutal punishment.[17]

During the 18th century the slave trade became a prominent institution in American life. Slavery flourished in the Southern colonies, but large numbers of slaves were also held in the Middle and New England colonies. Though the slave trade became much more institutionalized in the Southern states, slavers in New England were active as well. Newport, Rhode Island, for example, became a principal port of entry for the slave traders.

"The colony of Rhode Island, and in particular Newport, came to dominate the North American slave trade," wrote educator Fred Zilian in his story, *Rhode Island dominates North American Slave Trade in 18th Century:*

> "Even though it was the smallest of the colonies, the great majority of slave trips leaving British North America came from Rhode Island ports.[18]

> The voyage from New England to the West Indies for slaves ended with the infamous 'middle Passage' back to the New World again, and it became one of the major patterns of the 'triangular Trade'."

Slave importations mounted sharply after 1690. Virginia had 12,000 Black slaves by 1708 when it was importing about 1,000 a year. There were 23,000 in Virginia by 1715, 42,000 by 1743, 120,000 by 1756 and 260,000 by 1782. The importation of slaves in the colonies increased from an average of 2,500 a year between 1715 and 1750 to 7,500 on the eve of the American Revolution.[19]

By the time of the American Revolutionary War (1775-1783) slavery had been institutionalized in the United States. Though the word slavery was never used in the U.S. Constitution, it was an issue during its drafting.

Despite the efforts of some of the Founding Fathers to end slavery, those who were more conservative prevailed. They feared social disorder, political instability and economic chaos. The interests of the slaveowners were safeguarded by provisions for the return of runaway slaves and the extension of the slave trade:

> "The three-fifths compromise, by which five slaves were to be counted as three persons for purposes of taxation and representation...clearly indicates the strength of the pro-slaver interests at the Constitution Convention in Philadelphia in 1787."[20]

In a draft of the Declaration of Independence submitted to Congress in 1776, Jefferson included words from John Adams' vehement argument against slavery. The passages were stricken from the final version of the document.

As the brutality of slavery became ingrained in the American South's economy, so did the efforts Southern society to maintain protect it. Violent slave insurrections grew as the numbers running away to freedom increased. Such resistance signified continual deep-rooted discontent with the condition of bondage and resulted in ever-more-stringent mechanisms for social control and repression in slaveholding areas.[21]

The slave rebellions

In the United States, the myth of the contented slave became essential to the preservation of the South's "peculiar institution." But the increase of violent slave rebellions defied that image. Estimates of the total number of slave revolts vary according to the definition of insurrection. For the two centuries preceding the American Civil War, one historian found evidence of more than 250 uprisings or attempted uprisings involving 10 or more slaves.

The first large-scale conspiracy in the United States was conceived by Gabriel, an enslaved man in Virginia, in the summer of 1800. On August 30, more than 1,000 armed slaves massed for action near Richmond but were foiled by a violent rainstorm. The slaves were forced to disband, and 35, including Gabriel, were hanged.

The only free person to lead a rebellion was Denmark Vesey. Vesey's rebellion in 1822 reportedly involved as many as 9,000 slaves. But the conspiracy was betrayed before the plan could be put into effect. Some 130 Blacks were arrested and 35 (including Vesey) were hanged.

The third notable slave rebellion was led by Nat Turner, in Southampton County, Virginia. On August 21, 1831, Turner and a small band of slaves killed some 60 whites and attracted up to 75 slaves in the next few days. Hundreds of militia members and volunteers were able to stop the rebels near Jerusalem. They killed somewhere between 40 and 100. Turner was hanged.

A new wave of unrest spread through the South, accompanied by corresponding fear among slaveholders and the passage of more repressive legislation directed against both slaves and free Blacks. Those measures were aimed particularly at restricting the education of Blacks, their freedom of movement and assembly, and the circulation of inflammatory printed material.[22]

The Underground Railroad

A network to help Blacks escape the brutalities of slavery developed. Abolitionists and free Blacks provided food, shelter and money with the network of stations. The conductors, many of them runaway slaves themselves, serve as the conductors to lead the runaways to freedom in the North, Canada and even the Caribbean.

The runaway slaves moved mostly at night, hiding in the barns and homes of sympathetic whites and free Blacks. Two of the most famous of the conductors were Harriet Tubman and Josiah Henderson. It has been estimated that Tubman led 70 slaves to freedom in 13 trips back to the South, including her brothers, their wives and children and other relatives.

The slave codes

The infamous slave codes were enacted by the legislators in all of the slave states. It was a crime, punishable by a summary lashing, for an African to stand up straight and look a white man in the eye. It was a crime for slaves to hold meetings or religious services without a white witness. Slaves could not congregate in groups of more than two or three away from the home plantations. They could not beat drums, wear fine clothes or carry sticks as a weapon. They could not marry, they could not protect their children or their mates.[23]

State and federal governments, and all of U.S. presidents from Washington to Lincoln, stood behind these provisions. A huge police apparatus was created by the Southern states to enforce these repressive codes.

An economy built on slavery

These enforcements became even more necessary as slavery became an integral part of the American economy, especially the Southern states. The enslaved served as America's largest financial asset, and they were forced to maintain America's most exported commodity – cotton.

From 1801 to 1862, the amount of cotton picked daily by just one enslaved person increased 400 percent. The profits from cotton propelled the United States into one of the leading economies in the world and made the South its most prosperous region. The ownership of enslaved people increased wealth for Southern planters so much that by the dawn of the Civil War, the Mississippi River Valley had more millionaires per capita than any other region.[24]

The economic trajectory and development of capitalism in the United States are inextricably linked to the brutal institution of slavery. A paper by economist Mark Stelznar of Connecticut College and Sven Beckert of Harvard University showed how central this system of violence and forced labor was to the country's economic growth in the years leading up to the Civil War, which continues to shape racial inequities for Black Americans today.[25]

The authors' findings show that:

> "slavery was an important institution for economic development in the United States, and that the unrequited labor of enslaved women, men and children helped produce in significant ways the nation's economic expansion in the two decades before the Civil War."

Northern states had abolished slavery to some degree by 1805 – Vermont in 1777, Massachusetts in 1783, Connecticut and Rhode Island in 1784, New York in 1785, New Jersey in 1786, and Pennsylvania in 1789.

And though the import of slaves was banned by Congress in 1808, that law made smuggling common. But in the South the rapid expansion of the cotton industry after the invention of the cotton gin dramatically increased the need for slave labor. And the United States became even more polarized into "slave states" and free states.

Finally, emancipation

There were an estimated four million enslaved people when President Abraham Lincoln issued the Emancipation Proclamation in 1862. They were set free with virtually no help after generations of bondage and laws that denied them even a basic education.

Freedom, however, came at a heavy price. Hundreds of thousands died of hunger and disease after they were liberated. Historian Jim Downs in his book *Sick from Freedom*,[26] says emancipation during the chaos of the Civil War meant that the formerly enslaved suffered from rampant disease, including cholera and smallpox. Some died from starvation, while others, with nowhere to go, stayed on the plantations where they had been enslaved.

Downs's book is full of terrible vignettes about the individual experiences of slave families who embraced their freedom from the brutal plantations on which they had been born or sold to. Many ended up in encampments called "contraband camps" that were often near union army bases. However, conditions were unsanitary and food supplies limited. Shockingly, some contraband camps were actually former slave pens, meaning newly freed people ended up being kept virtual prisoners back in the same cells that had previously held them. In many such camps disease and hunger led to countless deaths. Often the only way to leave the camp was to agree to go back to work on the very same plantations from which the slaves had recently escaped.[27]

> "The slave system under which African Americans had been forced to live had not been designed to produce the independent, self-reliant citizens celebrated in nineteenth century American democratic political thought. Quite the contrary: it aimed to control every aspect of the lives of its black victims in order to extract maximum profits from their toil. The African Americans suddenly released from

bondage by the defeat of the Confederacy were thus impoverished, illiterate, and despised by most of the whites with whom they came into contact."[28]

New York Times journalist Hannah-Jones, in her preface to the book that grew out of *The 1619 Project*, wrote that slavery has been "whitewashed from American history."

Slavery historian Ira Berlin said in an essay, "The simple truth is that most Americans know little about the three-hundred-year history of slavery in mainland North America."[29]

It wasn't until March 3, 1865, that Congress established the Freedmen's Bureau to administer a program of social programs and self-help.

Officially named The Bureau of Refugees, Freedmen and Abandoned Lands, the Bureau was to supervise all relief and educational activities for the freedmen, including issuing rations, clothing and medicine. The Bureau was also tasked with operating hospitals in refugee camps. It was to take custody of all confiscated property in the former Confederate states, border states, Washington, D.C. and Indian territory.

On the same day in 1865 that the Freedmen's Bureau was established, Congress created the Freedman's Savings and Trust Company to help meet the financial needs of the newly freed Black people.

Black soldiers and veterans were to be to a primary target of the bank. Thousands of Black men, both freed and enslaved, had served in the Union Army and collected wages, some for the first time in their lives. But they had no place to keep their money and no way to send money home to their families. And many had no financial education or experience.

Many people think of the Civil War as the first time Blacks troops fought for the nation. Blacks soldiers, in fact, served and died fighting for the nation long before it became the United States America. But often they served in wars only as a last resort — when presidents and generals desperately needed more troops to put on the battlefields.

Chapter 3: Black soldiers fought for, and died for, America from the beginning

One of the primary reasons for the creation of the Freedman's Savings and Trust Company was to provide a place for Black Civil War veterans (and their widows) to save their wages, their enlistment bounties and their pensions.

Despite pervasive racism and discrimination on every level in American society, Blacks served – and died – in every U.S. war since the Revolution. In the Revolutionary War, Crispus Attucks, a Black man, was the first to die in the war when British troops fired on a group of protestors in the Boston massacre in 1770. Also, Black minutemen fought in the battle to defend the Concord Bridge in 1775 in Massachusetts.

Because of the enormous slave populations in the South (sometimes slaves outnumbered whites) there was a constant fear of slave uprisings. And thus, it became a major controversy as to whether Blacks, slaves or free, should bear arms in the Revolutionary War. In an effort to strengthen ties with the Southern states, the Continental Army issued an order to end recruitment or enlistment of Blacks. A measure was introduced in Congress to discharge all Blacks from the army. And though it was rejected, George Washington's war council terminated all African American enlistment weeks later. Congress later passed the law.[30] But after they realized that they badly needed more troops to fight the British, the rules excluding Black soldiers gradually ended. By the end of the war about 5,000 Blacks had been emancipated through military service.

According to U.S. Army records thousands of Black soldiers, both enslaved and free, from all 13 colonies, fought in the Continental Army during the American Revolution. Many also served in state militias.

"Black soldiers served in every major battle of the war, mostly in integrated units. A notable exception was America's first all-Black unit, the 1ˢᵗ Rhode Island Regiment. The regiment defeated three assaults by the British during the battle for Rhode Island in 1778 and later participated in the victory at Yorktown in 1781. About 20 percent of the tens of thousands of Blacks who served were freed from slavery as a result of their service."[31]

Though much of it is lost in American history, there were many other instances of Blacks who fought and died in the American revolution. *The Colored Patriots of the American Revolution,* by William Cooper Nell and with an introduction by Harriet Beecher Stowe, author of *Uncle Tom's Cabin,* was published in 1855.

The authors commended:

"the Colored Patriots of the American Revolution for fighting for a nation 'which did not acknowledge them as citizens and equals. It was not for their own land they fought, not even for a land which had adopted them, but for a land which had enslaved them, and whose laws, even in freedom, oftener oppressed than protected.'"[32]

Blacks soldiers also fought for the British, who promised them freedom. Some British generals later refused the demands of Americans to return the slaves who fought for them and instead boarded them on ships headed to England. Thomas Jefferson recounted that during the British retreat a large number of "Negroes, the property of inhabitants of the United States," were carried off in private vessels, avoiding inspection by American authorities.

Often overlooked in history are people who served the Americans in other ways, like James Armistead Lafayette, who working for the French, infiltrated the British under the guise of a runaway slave, and provided intelligence that proved critical to the French-

U.S. coalition victory and helped lead to the British surrender in 1781.

The War of 1812

The U.S. Army says that during the War of 1812, Black soldiers served in both integrated regiments as well as in all-black regiments, both on land and at sea.

Several northern states, including New York and Pennsylvania, recruited entire regiments of Black Soldiers. Even some southern states, like Louisiana and North Carolina, enlisted Black soldiers. Two battalions of Free Men of Color and several other units participated in the victory over the British during the Battle of New Orleans at the end of the War.[33]

The Civil War

Though the institution of slavery was never widespread in the Northern states and the slave trade was abolished by the U.S. Congress in 1808, the domestic slave trade not only grew, but it flourished. Over the next 50 years the enslaved population in the United States had tripled, growing to 4 million by 1860.[34]

The friction between the North and the South increased as the abolitionist movement grew in the North and the slave labor became ingrained in the South.

The conflict, years in the making, came to a head on November 8, 1860, when Abraham Lincoln and the Republican Party defeated Democratic nominee former general George B. McClellan by a wide margin. Lincoln and the Republican Party ran on an anti-slavery platform and won 55 percent of the popular vote and a landslide, 212-12, in the electoral college.

Even though Lincoln said he had no intention of ending slavery in the states where it existed, southerners were still outraged. By December 29, 1860, South Carolina seceded, followed by Mississippi, Florida, Alabama, Georgia, Louisiana and Texas by February 1, 1861.

The Civil War officially began when the newly created Confederacy attacked Fort Sumpter in Charleston, South Carolina on April 12, 1861. Following that attack, Virginia, Arkansas, North Carolina and Tennessee left the Union and joined the Confederacy.

Though Blacks had served on naval vessels for years, they did not serve in the army. And those who came forward and volunteered to serve were rejected. Lincoln upheld the 1782 law against Blacks enlisting in the army.

> "Still, many African Americans wanted to join the fighting and continued to put pressure on federal authorities. Even if Lincoln was not ready to admit it, blacks knew that this was a war against slavery. Some, however, rejected the idea of fighting to preserve a Union that had rejected them, and which did not give them the rights of citizens."[35]

Frederick Douglass had urged Lincoln to recruit Black soldiers, but the President resisted, believing white soldiers would not serve alongside Black soldiers.

The door finally opened to Blacks who wanted to serve when President Lincoln signed the Emancipation Proclamation in 1862. One of the reasons was that the Union needed more troops.

It wasn't until May 22, 1863, that the War Department created the Bureau of Colored Troops. By the end of the war roughly 179,000 Black men served in the U.S. Army as members of the U.S. Colored Troops, or about 10 percent of the Union Army. Another 19,000 served in the Navy, according to the National Archives.

Nearly 40,000 Black soldiers died during the war – 30,000 of them from disease or infection. Black soldiers served in artillery and infantry and performed all noncombat support functions that sustain an army, as well. Black carpenters, chaplains, cooks, guards, laborers, nurses, scouts, spies, steamboat pilots, surgeons, and teamsters also contributed to the war cause. There were nearly 80 Black commissioned officers. Black women, who could not formally join the Army, nonetheless served as nurses, spies, and scouts, the most famous being Harriet Tubman.[36] (One Black woman did serve. Cathay Williams joined the army in 1866 disguised as a man. She served until her true sex was discovered by an army doctor during an illness).

It was not smooth sailing for the Black troops. Black soldiers faced constant racism. Although many served in the infantry and artillery, discrimination relegated large numbers to non-combat, support duties as cooks, laborers, and teamsters.

They were paid $10 per month, from which $3 was deducted for clothing. The monthly pay of white soldiers was $13 per month, but no clothing allowance was deducted.

And if they were captured the Black soldiers faced a much greater threat from the Confederate Army.[37] In perhaps the most heinous example of abuse, Confederate soldiers shot to death black Union soldiers captured at the Fort Pillow, Tennessee, engagement in 1864. Confederate General Nathan B. Forrest witnessed the massacre and did nothing to stop it.[38]

Encouraged by Douglass, Blacks enlisted in large numbers once they were allowed to fight. The majority were slaves or former slaves from the South. A smaller percentage – maybe 20 percent – were from Northern states.

Perhaps the most famous of all the regiments was the 54th Massachusetts Volunteer Infantry, which was immortalized in the 1989 movie *Glory*, which starred Academy Award-winning actors Denzel Washington and Morgan Freeman. The 54th Massachusetts famously refused to accept the lower pay and served for months without pay until the government relented and agreed to pay them the same as the white soldiers.

Despite all the obstacles, the Black soldiers served valiantly. A third of them lost their lives.

Among the earliest Black regiments to fight in the war were Black regiments from New Orleans, the 1st and 3rd Louisiana Native Guards. According to journalist and Civil War historian Gary Rawlins, they were decimated in the battle in which the Union General Nathanial Banks lost 2,000 men in 1863, including 600 men from the two Black regiments. During that 45-day siege, the Union Army persevered and finally won control of the Mississippi River, but at a cost of 10,000 men, many to disease.

On July 6, Col. Robert Gould Shaw and the Massachusetts 54th led the assault on Battery Wagner, the strategic stronghold guarding Charleston Harbor. Though they fought gallantly, Shaw and many of the 54th lost their lives in the ensuing battle. More than 270 of the 650 men of the 54th that participated in the battle were killed, wounded, captured, or missing.[39]

History professor and Civil War expert Barbara Gannon, wrote that even though the movie *Glory* made Black military service part of the Civil War narrative, neither the movie nor previous scholarly studies[40] examined the unglamorous aftermath of the Civil War as experienced by Black American families,

> "including the mourning of loved ones who died in battle, the challenges of amputees who came home unable to work,

and the psychological toll of Black veterans whose minds never left a narrow beach under artillery fire."

Holly A. Pinheiro, Jr. in *The Families' Civil War, Black Soldiers and The Fight for Racial Justice,* focused on how Civil War service actually worsened conditions for the families of free Black citizens of Philadelphia. He said the race-based challenges of military service for Black Americans had a profound impact on Black families.

For example, Blacks in Philadelphia enlisted with the promise of monthly equal pay to white soldiers. What they found was that it was neither the same nor was it paid on time every month. Instead, they received $7 a month, as opposed to $13 dollars a month. And they were paid "whenever the Army mustered their unit for pay, theorctically, but not always, bimonthly." While this affected white soldiers, these men could also rely on bounties – bonuses for enlistment. But Black volunteers initially did not receive bonus payments. "Eventually, the government addressed these inequities, but Black families, who had always lived on the margin, were desperate by that time."[41]

Retired Lt. Colonel Jesse J. Johnson, in his 1969 book *The Black Soldier, documented 1619-1815,* says the true extent that Black slaves and freedmen were utilized as soldiers during that period will never be known, but "[h]istorically, the general practice of utilizing the Negro as a soldier may be characterized as the three R's: during peace, reject; during war, recruit; after war, reject."

World War I & beyond

About 380,000 Black soldiers served in World War I. More than one million Black men served in the armed forces in World War II. 600,000 served during the Korean War, including 5,000 who died. And 300,000 served in the Vietnam War, and more than 7,000 died – 12.4 percent of the total casualties.

In World War I Blacks were barred from the Marines and served only menial roles in the Navy. They were, however, able to serve in all branches of the Army except aviation. The 369th United States Infantry, nicknamed Harlem Hell Fighters, never lost a man, a trench or a foot of ground to the enemy. The regiment received the Croix de Guerre medal for its actions at the Maison-en-Champagne.

The Black soldiers who fought in World War II faced unequal treatment and limited opportunities. Black officers could only command Black troops. And if the soldiers left their bases in the U.S., they often faced hostility and discrimination.

Still, heroes emerged. Doris "Dorie" Miller, a Navy cook, was the first Black recipient of the Navy Cross and was nominated for a Medal of Honor after he shot down four to six Japanese planes during the attack on Pearl Harbor despite no gunnery training. He was nominated for a Medal of Honor, but never received it because of opposition by the Secretary of Navy who opposed Blacks serving in combat roles in the Navy. Miller died at age 24 when his ship was torpedoed by the Japanese in November 1943.

Segregation in the U.S. Armed Forces did not end until July 26, 1948, when President Harry Truman signed an executive order desegregating the services.

The late Gen. Colin Powell, the nation's first Black Chairman of the Joint Chiefs of Staff and the first Black Secretary of State, talked about his experiences with racism:

> "I came into the Army just after segregation ended, and it was still a situation where I could go to Fort Benning, Georgia, to get my infantry and paratroop and ranger training, but if I went outside of Fort Benning, Georgia, to Columbus, Georgia, it would still be segregated. I couldn't get a hamburger. And it was another few years before that

ended. So, we've come an extremely long way over the last half century of my public life, but there's a way to go yet. We shouldn't think it's over. We know it's not over."

After the Civil War ended, the Black veterans returned home to more challenges. There were few efforts to reward them for their valor and service. For some of the Black veterans, the end of the war meant a return to work on plantations in the South as men who were still not quite free.

President Lincoln and Congress created the Freedman's Bureau. But it was religious leaders, Union generals and abolitionists who fought for the creation of what eventually became the Freedman's Savings Bank.

Chapter 4: The war ended, bringing misery and chaos. But the Freedmen's Bureau brought help...and hope.

The American Civil War, also known as the War Between The States, ended on May 26, 1865. The number of men who died during the conflict is estimated at 750,000. But thousands of those deaths were from disease and infection, especially diarrhea and dysentery.

The Black soldiers suffered the same fate – maybe worse. Three quarters of them died from disease.

When the war ended, all hopes of a better life for the formerly enslaved were soon dashed. Instead, the end of the war brought chaos and despair.

Four million formerly enslaved people found themselves suddenly on their own, lacking housing, food or medical care. People who had never been on their own and had been legally denied any kind of education had no way to provide for themselves or their families. Their only hope was a Union Army that was not prepared, qualified or motivated to help.

At emancipation there were fewer than 500,000 free Blacks, or 12 percent of the nation's Black population. Half, or about 261,000, lived in the South; 226,000 lived in the North.[42]

But it was the formerly enslaved Blacks who were facing Herculean tasks of survival. For many, it did not end well. Historian Jim Downs, professor of Civil War Studies and History at Gettysburg College and author of *Sick from Freedom,* said the newly freed slaves suffered immensely. Disease was rampant, and the population was savaged by outbreaks of smallpox and cholera. Hundreds of thousands died.

Downs recounted some shocking accounts of the deplorable conditions faced by the freed slaves in make-shift hospitals and refugee camps.

> "Things were so bad that one military official in Tennessee in 1865 wrote that the formerly enslaved were: 'dying by scores – that sometimes 30 per day die and are carried out by wagonloads without coffins, and thrown promiscuously, like brutes, into a trench'."[43]

It wasn't until March 3, 1865, that Congress established the Freedmen's Bureau. The goal was to administer social and self-help programs. The new agency was tasked with administering clothing and rations and operating hospitals and refugee camps.

Despite corruption and outright hostility from whites in the Southern states, including and especially President Andrew Johnson, who assumed the presidency after Lincoln's assassination, the Bureau was relatively successful in providing the freed Blacks with supplies and medical care. It also provided free transportation to the formerly enslaved so they could find employment.

When Congress introduced a bill in February 1866 to extend the Bureau's tenure and give it new legal powers, Johnson vetoed it on the grounds that it interfered with states' rights, gave preference to one group of citizens over another and would impose a huge financial burden on the federal government, among other issues.[44]

Bureau agents, who acted essentially as social workers, were frequently the only federal representatives in Southern communities. They were often subjected to hostility and violence from whites, including the Ku Klux Klan.

The Freedmen's Bureau fed millions of former slaves, built hospitals, provided medical aid and even negotiated labor contracts for ex-slaves. It also helped former slaves legalize marriages and locate lost relatives. And it provided much-needed assistance for Black Civil War veterans.

Perhaps the greatest success of the Bureau was in education. Howard University in Washington, D.C., Hampton Institute (now Hampton University) in Hampton, Virginia, Atlanta University in Atlanta, Georgia and Fisk University in Nashville, Tennessee were among the schools established during the period which received assistance from the Freedmen's Bureau.[45]

Maya Rockeymoore Cummings, a consultant and politician, and the widow of the later Congressman Elijah Cummings says after slavery there was an opportunity to help repair the wrongs of slavery through the programs of Freedman's Bureau, which was offering assistance in education banking and economic security. But strong resistance from whites made it difficult if not impossible:

> "And there was active white hostility to that agenda. There was an organized effort to basically undermine the Freedmen's Bureau and basically undo the compensatory structure of the post slavery reconstruction, including a direct assault on voting rights."

Despite its successes, in the summer of 1872, Congress, partly responding to pressure from white Southerners and President Johnson, dismantled the Freedmen's Bureau.

The Freedman's Bank

On the same day in 1865 that the Freedmen's Bureau was established, Congress created the Freedman's Savings and Trust Company to help meet the financial needs of the newly freed Black people. Thousands of freed and enslaved Blacks had served in the Union Army and collected wages, some for the first time in their lives. But they had no place to save their money. And they had no financial education or experience.

The need for the bank's services was acute. Both freedmen and slaves joined the Union Army and were on its payroll. For some it was the first money they had ever earned. They needed a safe depository, but they also needed basic financial education, which was a goal of the Freedman's Bank. Another goal of the bank was employment for freedmen, in jobs that would give them hands-on training and banker's skills.

After the Civil War a number of abolitionists were promoting the establishment of a bank that would serve the needs of the formerly enslaved. John W. Alvord, a minister, and Anson M. Sperry, a U.S. Army paymaster, led the effort in New York in 1865. Separately, there was an effort in South Carolina to do the same thing.

Those two initiatives were combined and provided the foundation for the formation of the bank.

Carl Osthaus, professor emeritus at Oakland University wrote:

> "The beginning was auspicious. On January 27, 1865, while the Union and Confederate armies fought before Richmond, twenty-two New York businessmen, philanthropists, and humanitarians met in the directors' room of the American Stock Exchange Bank to discuss the establishment of a savings institution for Negro soldiers. It was the Reve. John W. Alvord, teacher, Congregational minister, and longtime abolitionist who had summoned this gathering of prominent New Yorkers..."[46]

The group of prominent New Yorkers Alvord pulled together was impressive. There was Peter Cooper, a manufacturer and philanthropist and William Cullen Bryant, the abolitionist editor of the *New York Evening Post*. Other prominent businessmen in the group were Abraham Baldwin, R.R. Graves, Walter T. Hatch and

A.S. Hatch, all businessmen. A.S. Barnes was a publisher who was also involved in the railroad, banking and insurance industries. Hiram Barney was a well-known and respected attorney and Republican politician.[47]

The group of businessmen and philanthropists voted unanimously to support the creation of a savings bank to promote "thrift" among the newly freed Negroes. This permanent civilian bank was to replace those temporary military banks that were created to help the Black soldiers save their money and support their families back home.

A second meeting was held on Feb. 1, 1865, at which a tentative incorporation was created for discussion at the next meeting. At the third meeting, five days later, the group decided to send Alvord and Rev. George Whipple of the American Missionary Association to Washington to promote the bank to politicians, government officials and Chief Justice Salmon Chase, an early supporter of the creation of a bank that would cater to the Black Americans.

At the fourth meeting the businessmen received a report from Whipple that there was support from Congressmen and members of the president's cabinet, and that Senator Henry Wilson of Massachusetts had, in fact, already introduced legislation to create the bank. The group sent Alvord and Whipple back to Washington to lobby for the bill.[48]

Their efforts resulted in Congressional legislation that was passed on March 3, 1865, creating the Freedman's Savings and Trust Company as a nonprofit financial institution. The legislation was signed into law by President Abraham Lincoln.

According to the charter, money deposited was to be invested in "stocks, bonds, Treasury notes, or other securities of the United

States."[49] But unlike conventional banks, the Freedman's Bank was forbidden to make loans. Instead, it was designed to operate as a cooperative; depositors owned a share of the bank's assets in proportion to their deposits. A board of 50 trustees, all white men, was named to manage the bank.

Osthaus wrote that the strongest feature of the charter was the board of 50 trustees. In fact, he said it would be difficult to find in 1865 a group of men better known for their business and financial acumen, antislavery principles and philanthropy. "Their names read like an abbreviated who's who of American life."

There was Cooper and Bryant; William Claflin, a congressman and future governor of Massachusetts and founder and president of a Boston national bank; George S. Coe, president of the American Exchange Bank, probably the nation's foremost authority of finance. The strength prestige of the group of businessmen was probably one of the reasons Congress approved the charter.

Still, the group included no Blacks and no women, and none of these trustees lived in Washington, D.C., where Congress intended the bank to be based.

The New York Times said the bank would be a "cheap, valuable and welcome boon for the freedmen for whose benefit it is designed."

Over the next few months, the trustees elected officers, selected agents and established a home office in New York City. They also expanded into the south and established branches – all without any funds. The trustees elected William A. Booth, a prominent New York banker, as president. Mahlon T. Hewitt, a New York businessman, was elected first vice president, and Walter L. Griffith, was elected second vice president. Alvord was elected corresponding secretary.

The Office of the Comptroller of the Currency was created in 1863, two years before the Freedman's Bank. The office was responsible for supervising the banks it chartered. Real estate lending was prohibited.

But the Freedman's Bank was established in a way that its depositors did not have the same safeguard. Congress subjected the bank's charter not to the Office of the Comptroller of the Currency, but to Congress itself.

U.S. Rep. Kweisi Mfume said the bank started out as a noble idea, "probably out of a sense of guilt":

> "They were hoping that if it was successful, it would bring about some sense of stability financially, in the communities, the towns and the hamlets where so many of these ex-slaves found themselves."

Alvord's plan was not the first to try to help the Black soldiers and veterans save. Several Northern states had systems that allowed soldiers, both Black and white, to have a portion of their monthly pay deducted from their checks and sent to relatives or to be held by the military until they left the service.

Alvord, though, was not only critical to the bank's creation, but he was also critical to the bank's expansion and early success. A minister, teacher and abolitionist, he also became superintendent of schools and finances for the Freedman's Bureau.

A Civil War army chaplain, Alvord traveled with the Army of the Potomac during the 1861-1864 Virginia campaigns. He may be best known for a series of letters he wrote from the south on the state of the freedmen during that time and his later time at the Freedman's Bureau.

Meanwhile, New York City was selected as the headquarters for the bank and Alvord and the officers opened the home office in

May. Using his extensive network in the missionary community, he traveled extensively through the south in the early years after the bank officially began operations, opening branches and hiring cashiers.

The plan to provide a safe place for Black soldiers to deposit their pay was key. It was evident from the time they entered the army that they needed help to save their money:

> "For both Black and white troops, payday was a time of reckless extravagance when gamblers, prostitutes and confidence men descended on the camps to fleece the troopers. Even some unscrupulous officers joined the raid."[50]

In addition, the soldiers were paid a bounty, usually about $100, to enlist in the Union Army. And the soldiers and their families were eligible to receive U.S. government pensions.

Some military commanders had also tried to assist the Black soldiers. In 1864 Gen. Rufus Saxton created the Military Savings Bank at Beaufort, South Carolina, which eventually became the South Carolina Freedmen's Savings Bank. After only a year the bank had $180,000 in funds, mostly from the formerly enslaved. Gen. Benjamin Butler created a bank in Norfolk, Virginia the same year. Gen. Nathaniel Banks started the Free Labor Bank in Louisiana, which held deposits of thousands of Black soldiers and former slaves.[51]

At the end of the war there were tens of thousands of dollars of unclaimed deposits of Black soldiers who had disappeared or had died without leaving surviving relatives. The Freedman's Bank was established, in part, as a depositor for those unclaimed funds.

The initial plan, according to Hollis Gentry Brown, at Smithsonian Libraries and Archives in Washington, D.C was:

"to take the funds from the soldiers who were missing in action or who were deceased, or whom they couldn't locate after the war, the funds that they were due from the bounty, the pay, or pensions."

While these efforts to create military banks had limited success, Alvord thought of them as temporary measures. A permanent savings bank was needed if the former slaves and the Black war veterans were to make a successful transition from slavery to freedom and to be truly incorporated into the economic mainstream of American society.[52]

Both Black and white veterans were eligible for a pension. The dollar amount depended on the degree of disability, regardless of the veteran's employment status, his job if employed, or his wealth. Application was through a pension attorney, and the degree of disability was determined by a board of three local doctors employed by the Pension Bureau and following guidelines established by the bureau.[53]

Gentry Brown started researching the bank to find out more about her ancestor, Daniel Langley, from Norfolk, Virginia, who served with the 2nd U.S. Colored Troops Infantry in the Civil War. He was her second great uncle – brother of her great, great grandfather.

She found his information in the bank records and pension records. Those files showed that he found success as a shoemaker after the war and became a prominent member of the Black community in Norfolk and was a member of an organization called The Star of Bethlehem.

Langley had a brother, Nickolas Langley, who had also served in the U.S. Colored Troops. After the war the family attained some level of prominence and was well known in the Norfolk Black community, she said.

Records at the U.S. National Archive have information on hundreds of other soldiers. For example, Washington Hendley, a Civil War veteran, transferred his account from Norfolk, Virginia to Richmond on May 6, 1868. He served in the 36th U.S. Colored Troops, Company D in Texas. He had deposited $100, that with dividends brought his savings to $105.05.[54]

But if Black soldiers and veterans were the original target base of the bank, former slaves, veterans, farmers, businessmen and women, maids, churches and even children opened accounts. It quickly grew to be a nationwide bank in the view of the depositors.

The Freedman's Bank came to view it as America's "Black" bank. And the depositors thought that it was a safe place to deposit their hard-earned money. They were soon to find out that neither was true.

They were also about to become a part of an ugly stain in the nation's history books that would change the lives of Black Americans for generations to come.

Chapter 5: The Freedman's Bank grows. But did it grow too big, too fast?

Things started slowly for the Freedman's Savings Bank. Some of those early struggles were an ominous sign of the troubles that would come later. As impressive as the group of 50 (all-white) trustees was, there were later questions about whether they actually had the time (or the experience) to oversee the bank adequately.

There was no working capital. In fact, the trustees asked the board members each to lend the bank $100 to help get the bank going. Some complied, others did not.

There was a major marketing campaign to encourage African Americans to deposit money into the bank. The Smithsonian's Gentry Brown discussed the misleading way in which they advertised in local newspapers. They had pictures of Lincoln and other leaders who were known to be associated with emancipation or freedom:

> "So, for the African American community, looking from the outside in, it appeared as if the Freedmen's bank was part of the Freedmen's Bureau and therefore, a lot of people believed that the funds were secured by the federal government. And they thought perhaps that the same government that had just freed them was also really invested in helping them to become citizens."

It was generally and erroneously believed that funds deposited in the bank were protected by the U.S. government. This misconception was systematically propagated by the managers of the bank.

A U.S. Senate committee later agreed. That report said the passbooks' covers featured President Lincoln, General Grant and others who the freedmen saw as benefactors as well as the American flag.

The campaign seemed to work, especially among the Black soldiers and veterans. The bank was ready for business.

Despite the lack of working capital, the trustees felt a network of branches was necessary, particularly in the South. That, however, was not the intent of Congress. The original intent by Congress was to specify that the bank have only one branch, in Washington, D.C. That was somehow lost in the rush to pass the legislation. Instead, the bank's administrators made plans to establish branches in Washington, D.C., Norfolk, Virginia and Richmond, Virginia. Norfolk was the first to open, in June 1865, perhaps because it was where General Butler's military savings bank was located.[55]

Alvord traveled to Norfolk and called a meeting of the city's leading Black clergymen at the St. John's African Methodist Church. The Black local leaders agreed on the need for a branch, but insisted that their own candidate, a Black man with no experience in banking and finance, be installed as cashier. Alvord overruled the locals and installed two white men as cashier and assistant cashier.

Washington, D.C., the center of efforts to help the freedmen, was the bank's second branch. Not only did it have a sizable Black population, but it was also near a large concentration of Black troops.

After meeting with a group of Black businessmen, Alvord and Hewitt appointed an advisory committee and commissioned a Black teacher, William J. Wilson, as cashier. He was also tasked with promoting the bank to the city's Black community.[56]

The branch struggled along for the first few months. Its office, if such it could be called, was located in the upper story of a brick house on G Street and was open only in the evenings. Cashier Wilson, who received no compensation for his work, gave the bank what time he could spare from his full-time position with the schools. Because of the bank's newness as well as the heritage of slavery, Wilson encountered distrust and prejudice in his first efforts to teach adult freedmen.[57]

Next up was the Norfolk branch. Alvord and Hewitt traveled to Norfolk and called a meeting of 60 to 70 Black community representatives. This group appointed a committee to canvass the community to determine its sentiment on supporting the creation of a local bank branch. That canvassing proved successful, and the Richmond branch opened for operation in mid-October.

Alvord and Hewitt then sent representatives throughout the south to promote the bank. And with that came the bank's crusade against poverty and for education and financial literacy among the nation's Black population.

By the end of that first year the bank had added seven more branches. And in less than two years it had expanded to 22 branches, all in cities with sizable Black populations – Baltimore, Charleston, New Orleans and Savannah, Georgia, for example. Branches were later established in smaller cities likes Vicksburg, Mississippi and Houston, Texas, again, near where Black soldiers were stationed, in hopes that they would attract the deposits of bounty money from the Black soldiers.

Whether that was part of the plan or not, the bank was growing into a giant morass of branches that was somewhat unprecedented at the time.

As Osthaus wrote:

"Knowingly or unknowingly, the trustees and officers had created a miniature financial empire, in the early years more impressive in extension than in fiscal strength."

Despite the impressive growth, the bank was struggling financially. Maintaining such a huge branch system was very expensive and it was virtually impossible to manage and oversee.

The Freedman's Savings Bank could not afford to pay employees a living wage, paying only $60 to $125 per month to cashiers and assistant cashiers (what communities paid teachers). That meant the bank had virtually no chance of hiring experienced bankers.[58]

Therein was one of the initial problems. The cashiers had no banking experience. Also, the bank was largely hiring workers with missionary rather than banking or accounting experience. Others were recruited from the Black communities and from the Freedmen's Bureau. The Washington cashier, for example, had trouble balancing the books. The Chattanooga cashier frantically asked the main office for help understanding the books. In Charleston, the cashier had a discrepancy that could not be found.[59]

According to some documents, Alford thought the cashier in Raleigh was the most incompetent bookkeeper of all the branches. However, there were no details on his performance or what made him the worst in Alvord's eyes. Recognizing the enormous problems, Alvord proposed that the cashiers be bonded and be required to hold monthly meetings with the local advisory board. It's not clear if those proposals were ever put into effect.

As the bank's footprint grew, expenses exceeded income. Some branches in small cities had no chance of ever becoming profitable. Adding to the problems, the army's Black regiments were beginning to be discharged and sent home. Bank administrators were considering closing some of the weaker branches, even entirely shutting down the bank. Instead, salaries were cut. The 22 branches attracted 70,000 depositors, many with savings in the range of $1 to $50.

The Freedman's Bank moved its operations to Washington, D.C. in 1867 and built a headquarters at the southeast corner of Lafayette Square at a cost of more than $200,000 to construct and furnish.[60]

Ultimately there were 37 branches in 17 states and the District of Columbia. You only needed five cents to open an account in those days.

Blacks were also beginning to be hired to work at the bank, according to the U.S. Treasury Department's history of the bank. By 1874, nearly half of the bank's employees were Black. Most were cashiers – the top officials at the branches. Otherwise, they were assistant cashiers, clerks, or messengers.

Though most of those branches were in former slave states in the South, there were branches in Northern cities. The Branch network extended as far north as New York, Philadelphia and Baltimore, as far south as Jacksonville and Tallahassee, Florida and as far west as St. Louis. There were also branches in New Orleans and Houston.

According to Yannelis of The University of Chicago, at its height the bank provided financial services to approximately one in seven Blacks living in the 19th Century U.S. South. Documents show that a large number of African Americans were using the services of the bank to purchase real estate, start businesses and pay educational expenses both for themselves and their children.

Rep. Mfume said the number of branches increased because the ex-slaves responded to the Freedman's Bank. Nothing like it had existed in their lifetimes. Also, it was the first time they could actually bank.

It was a key step in legitimizing their freedom, said Brandon K. Winford, associate professor of history at the University of Tennessee-Knoxville and author of *John Harvey Wheeler, Black Banking and The Economic Struggle for Civil Rights*:

> "For Black people coming into their freedom for the first time and that focus on political democracy and the right to vote, economic democracy for them was an important step in actualizing, their freedom. So, understanding what economic viability, what economic freedom actually looked like for them, the Freedmen's Bank opened up the possibilities of shoring up land ownership, thinking about saving for a house saving for the children and paying for their children's education."

The Black Civil War veterans were the depositors most sought after by the bank, particularly as it expanded in the early years. The bulk of the first deposits in the branches was comprised of the back pay and bounty money of these soldiers. Bank cashiers worked closely with Freedmen's Bureau distribution officers, who were solely responsible for distributing the back pay and bounties of the Black soldiers.[61]

John Alvord by this time served as president of the bank while he also served general superintendent of education of the Freedmen's Bureau. Many felt that this close relationship with the Freedmen's Bureau added to the Black depositors' belief that the Freedman's Bank was a federal government institution.

The bank's administrators did everything they could to convince Blacks that their money was not only safe, but they tried to infer that it was backed by the federal government, which it was not. Passbooks and other bank literature contained numerous slogans and poems on temperance, frugality, economy, chastity, the virtues of thrift & savings.

Promotional materials cited the names of Abraham Lincoln and other government officials. The bank, however, was under the charter of Congress, which was somewhat misleading. Congress had the right to inspect the books, but it never did. In fact, there was virtually no outside supervision.

The bank advertised extensively, more so than other financial institutions at the time. A number of newspapers, both Black and white, wrote stories about the bank. But the bank's advertising relied on false promises. The bank promoted itself as benefiting from a government guarantee as reflected by a bank circular in 1865.

> "Being a National Institution ...it is as safe as the Government can make it, and therefore, there can be no safer place in the country to deposit."[62]

With assurances (however hollow) that their money was safe, Blacks from all backgrounds began to open accounts at a phenomenal rate between 1868 and 1874 – farmers, laborers, cooks, janitors, nurses and porters.

Civil War veterans were among the most active in opening accounts. For many Blacks, since it was the first time in their lives that they were receiving wages and handling money, so a bank account was a source of pride and excitement.[63]

For Gentry Brown, of the Smithsonian, the assumption that most Blacks were ignorant on financial matters and never handled money was not necessarily true:

> "They're the people who were serving in supporting roles for the people who enslaved them, who handled their businesses, who handled operations.

"It's not that African Americans were unfamiliar with banking. It's just that legally, it was not widespread for the enslaved population."

Still, she said, the bank had appeal, and for Blacks it became a matter of prestige to have an account.

"There were some observers who noticed that freedmen would get dressed up to go to the bank to make the deposit, even though they might be depositing only a few pennies."

In New York City, 7-year-old **Samuel William Kemp**, of 87 Thompson St., opened an account (#1614) on Nov. 14, 1870. A student at Spring Street School, he listed his father's name as William and his mother as "Mrs. Cook." (His real mother had died years before). He lists two siblings, Henrietta Cook and Martha Cook.

Children were also encouraged to make deposits and cashiers routinely preached to them about the importance of work and saving. The schoolchildren opened accounts for as little as five cents to as much as twenty-five cents. At the Augusta, Georgia branch nearly twenty-five percent of the depositors were children. [64] [65]

Black churches, private businesses, and social groups also opened accounts. They often took the lead in making deposits and were the driving force behind getting many individual depositors to open accounts.

A newspaper reporter in Charleston, Carolina in 1870 wrote:

"Go in any forenoon and the office is found full of Negroes depositing little sums of money, drawing little sums, or remitting to a distant part of the country where they have relatives to support or debts to discharge." [66]

Prof. Brandon K. Winford says, in fact, that the bank was successful for a number years.

"From about 1865 to about 1872, when they amended the charter, you could argue that it was successful in terms of

Black people were supporting this financial institution with their fund, with their dollars."

One of the scholars, Carl Osthaus (author of *Freedmen, Philanthropy and Fraud*) says that The Freedman's Bank does become a Black bank for all practical purposes, because you had domestics, farmers, laborers and African Americans across the board, putting their money into their institution.

William Green, a 7-year-old born in Hamburg, South Carolina, opened an account in the on January 27, 1871. He attended a school in the city. He listed his parents, Monroe and Clarissa, three uncles (Henry, Reuben, and Jack) and three aunts (Patsy, Amy, and Emmeline) as relatives. His mother, who washed and cooked to earn a living, opened a separate account on July 20, 1872.

All kinds of intimate information can be found in the hundreds of passbooks saved in the National Archives in Washington, D.C. and College Park, Maryland.

The Home Mission Society of Orchid Street Station opened an account in the Baltimore, Maryland branch on May 17, 1867, with $100. Keepers of the account, the banking committee, was comprised of Mrs. Elisa A. Hogan, Mrs. Hasoich A. Abrames and Mrs. Sidney Barnes.

The bank also was a depository for their military pensions, which the administrators lobbied hard to receive. That included pensions that were supposed to go to the widows of deceased Civil War soldiers. Many times, the widows had to go through an arduous and difficult pension application process that could be both racist and humiliating – sometimes having to answer questions about sexual reputation and infidelity – only to be rejected.

Joseph Haskins, former CEO of Harbor Bank in Baltimore says:

"It was a noble effort made to create an avenue for African Americans to be able to deposit money and to build some wealth."

The success of the scheme was demonstrated by the number of depositors that it was able to gain and the number of states that it was able to operate in: "It was the right thing to do, and it brought to the attention of those who weren't thinking about how to save their money, the importance of doing so."

King Solomon Lodge No. 4 at 8th Avenue and 14th Street in New York City opened an account on Nov. 12, 1870 (Account #1588). Lewis Willitt was one of three names on the account as an authorized user. He was 46, "dark brown" complexion, and lived at 36 ½ Comelia St. with his wife Mary Ann and six children. The other authorized signature on the account was Joseph Augustus Thompson, 36, complexion: dark brown, who was born in Brooklyn. He had a wife and two young children.

The bank's organizers, especially Alvord, had deep-rooted beliefs in the bank's missionary crusade. Alvord believed the bank's purpose was to turn the "ignorant" freedmen into morally upright citizens. And they expected the cashiers to also serve as ministers, or preachers.

Alvord's advice to the cashiers:

"I need not say, what you know so well by experience, that our work in this first period of our history, is missionary – almost religiously so…How, then, to occupy both the counter and pulpit – be Cashier and preacher…"[67]

The bank's cashiers went out into the Black community to drum up support. Some lectured at Black churches and worked to make Black teachers believers so they could promote savings among the young students.

Every piece of Freedman's Bank literature revealed the officers' missionary zeal. Bank officials incessantly distributed, in the words of the Bank's actuary, D.L. Eaton, "tracts and papers…on temperance, frugality, economy, chastity, the virtues of thrift & savings..."[68]

The Washington, D.C.-based *National Era* (a crusading anti-slavery Black weekly newspaper founded by J. Sella Martin, a former slave) published this advertisement every week from June 1871 to July 1873.

Stephen Brown, a 49-old farmer, opened an account on January 21, 1871, at the branch in Augusta, Georgia. Born in the Barnwell District of South Carolina, he lived in Land Hills, Georgia, with his wife, Henrietta. His son, Wilson Brown, apparently "went off" after Emancipation. His mother and father were recorded as Hetty Jacob and Nixon Brown (dead). Also listed were three brothers: Sam Flowers (dead), Dick Brown, and Brister Brown (dead).

"Cut off your vices – don't smoke – don't drink – don't buy lottery tickets. Put your money in the Freedman's Savings Bank."[69]

But even as the Freedman's Bank's grew and expanded, it was struggling financially. Overhead costs were extremely high. It was costly to maintain so many branches. Also, the bank's source of income was limited. Its profits came from investing depositors' money in government bonds, which did not pay much.

Gentry Brown said the people who were running the bank had good intentions, but they had no idea what they were doing. Many had no banking skills whatsoever. That's the reason the bank failed the way it did.

"Looking at the cohort of people who started the organization, who eventually ran the organization, many, many of them had no banking skills that would have ensured the success of that bank."

The Freedman's Bank had become a trusted and respected institution in the Black community. The passbook became a badge of honor.

Black civic groups, churches, business owners, farmers and laborers trusted the bank with their wages and their savings. Parents took their children – young and old – to open passbook accounts.

Mary Jane Johnson (passbook #5554) opened an account at the Bank branch in Augusta, Georgia on June 8, 1873, with $40. With interest payments ranging from $1 to $2 and another deposit of $20, she ended up with a total of $52.03 in April 1875.

That all made it even more devastating when the news came that the bank was in trouble.

When the end finally came, it was clear that the depths of the problems had been long-lasting and deep rooted. And the incompetence and corruption converged with a worldwide financial crisis meant disaster for the bank, and to its thousands of Black depositors.

When the bank closed, however, many of the civic organizations, particularly the churches and beneficial societies, had to suspend or drastically curtail vital services, thus adding to the social and economic woes of the African American community.

In his book, Osthaus described the confusion and devastation as depositors in Black communities near the bank's branches heard the news of the bank's failure.

"Hundreds of freedmen ran directly to their branch offices, asking anxiously if the rumor were true. When told that the bank had suspended and would begin paying its depositors soon, almost all – with complaints and lamentation – acquiesced in the fait accompli, for there was little that they could do.

"Meanwhile, depositors across the South petitioned Congress, pleading that the government assume the bank's assets and reimburse the depositors. These petitions revealed that, by late 1874, the depositors were becoming suspicious that the liquidation of the bank was coming, adding yet another story of betrayal of trust to the dismal record. They suspected the commissioners of mismanagement."[70]

It was not clear if people outside of the bank – white or Black – knew how deeply the bank had become ingrained in Black communities where it had branches – mostly in the North and South.

Farmers could not buy seeds plant their crops. Parents could not send their children to school. Children lost the little savings that could have made a difference in their life.

A closer look at who the depositors were tells the story of just how hard the nascent Black community was hit when the bank that they took so much pride in suddenly and finally closed its doors.

Chapter 6: A closer look at the bank's depositors

There is a surprising trove of information and scholarly research on the Freedman's Bank, even though it collapsed 150 years ago. Those records reveal valuable information on the people who opened accounts.

Washington Hendley, (mother's name Mary) had served in the 36th U.S. Colored Troops, Company D. He opened his account originally in Texas Sept. 5, 1865, and later moved it to Norfolk. He had his savings, $105.05, transferred to the Freedman's branch in Richmond, on May 6, 1868. By then he was a farmer.

Thousands of pages of information, including internal documents, correspondence, depositor applications and even passbooks are available at the National Archives in Washington, D.C. and College Park, Maryland. In addition, the Church of the Latter-Day Saints made the records available to millions through the creation of an easily accessible database.

The bank was created and originally catered to the Black soldiers who volunteered to fight in the Civil War, both the formerly enslaved and the freedmen who had no place to hold their cash and no way to send money home to their families.

The reach of the bank grew quickly, and before long the bank's customers included Blacks of all ages and occupations, including farmers, teachers, homemakers, tradesmen and school children. Clubs and civic organizations and churches also opened accounts at what they thought was a Black bank. Howard University had an account.

Professor Brandon K. Winford points out that being an accountholder at the Freedman's Bank was important as a statement of a person's personal and economic identity "They could document their newfound freedom. They were forced to submit paperwork. They were forced to submit documentation. So, it opened up and established their freedom right in real time through kind of documentation."

Jacob Reiley, a 22-year-old who had served with Company B of the 33rd United States Colored Troops, opened an account at the Savannah, Georgia, branch on April 6, 1866. Although living in Screven County at the time he opened his account, he was born in Augusta, Georgia, where he was owned by Josiah Sibley. His signature records indicated that when he served in the army, he had been a cook for General Sherman.

Most of the deposits were small, $50 or less. Accounts could be opened with as little as a nickel, and deposits as small as $1 were able to earn interests. "People would often put their money in the bank during the summer and autumn and take it out in the winter and spring, when their supplies would be running low. People also used their savings to buy bigger items such as homes, land, farm animals and tools."[71]

Early on the bank requested detailed personal information, especially from the formerly enslaved, including their former owners, and family members. They even required depositors' information on skin tone.

For example, one depositor who has been written about often is Dilla Warren, 50, widow of a Black Civil War soldier Oscar Warren. Oscar had served with the U.S. Colored Troops infantry, Regiment 36, Company and died in an army hospital on Dec. 1, 1864 of pleurisy.[72]

Warren opened an account at the New Bern, North Carolina, branch on November 2, 1869. Her signature records not only provide an interesting example of the value of the Freedman's Bank records for genealogical research but also give a tragic example of the effect slavery had on the stability of the African American family.[73]

Born in Chowan County, North Carolina. She made her living from sewing, knitting, washing, and ironing despite being crippled. Her first husband, Pompey Nixon, was "sold away" seventeen years before the Civil War.

Her signature records list eleven of her fifteen children, including those who either died or were sold. Warren's father, Ned Clark, was sold thirty years before the Civil War. Her mother, Harriet Nixon, along with her two brothers, Ned and Allen, was sold seventeen years before the war. Another brother, Andrew M., was killed by lightning. Warren's signature records also provide the names of her two sisters, Ann Carter (sold thirty-five years before Warren opened her account) and Maria Gregory.[74]

Another former slave who opened an account was James Clinket, who deposited $225 in the Washington, D.C. branch on January 27, 1866. Born in King George County, Virginia, his former owners were Pinsett and Louisa Taylor. According to his account records, he and his wife, Julia, had three children: Mary S., Patsy, and Isaac.

Clinket was among several depositors at the District of Columbia branch who listed their residence as Freedmen's Village, one of the contraband camps established in the Washington, D.C. area in the early 1860s under the jurisdiction of the War Department. The villages served as refuge for thousands of fugitive slaves and other destitute freedmen.[75]

The background and biographical information was much more complete on the earlier account deposit applications.

"For example, the blank form in the beginning asked for the name of the slave master and slave mistress and that kind of information," says Gentry Brown. "Towards the end, when the accounts were opened after the passage of the 13th Amendment, when there were no enslaved people or they were a little bit more removed from slavery, they didn't ask for that information."

> **Samuel William Kemp,** aged 7, had an account opened by his stepmother, "Mrs. Cook," on November 14, 1870. His birth mother had died years earlier. His father, stepmother and a brother and sister lived at 87 Thompson St. in New York, and he attended Spring Street School. The accounted listed his complexion as "dark brown."

Gentry Brown says she had multiple forebears/ancestors who had accounts at the Freedman's Bank, including her third great grandfather on her father's side, also a Civil War veteran.

"It appears that the paymaster or officer in his regiment deposited his bounty pay in the bank. And he withdrew that money, purchased land and that land deeded the beginning of a community in Kentucky that now named after him."

Eventually, as the bank grew, depositors expanded to include immigrant groups and even some whites in Northern cities searching for higher interest on their savings.

> **Josiah** and **Jane Allen** of Woodford County, Kentucky opened an account for their 15-year-old son, Josiah Allen Jr. in Louisville, Kentucky on Jan. 6, 1872. The initial deposit was $11.02.

"There are depositors in the bank who were immigrants, European immigrants and Caribbean immigrants, who deposited a considerable amount of money," said Gentry Brown.

Malcolm Wardlaw (Associate Professor, Department of Finance at Terry College of Business) said rates on deposits reached 6 percent ("a reasonably generous return on deposits"). The Freedman's Savings Bank began to attract white depositors, especially in New York. "And so, by the early 1870s, more than 10 percent (up to 13 percent to 14 percent) of the depositor base was white depositors," he said.

Josiah Sr., 42, opened an account for himself at the same Louisville branch, listing his occupation as carpenter and his parents' names as Wickliffe Bob and Melvina.

The First African Baptist Church of Richmond, Virginia opened an account in 1870. Trustees were **James D. Allen**, **G. B. Anderson**, **John Randolph**, **Nelson P. Vanderwall** and **Benjamin Harris**, secretary.

"The bank accounts for the New York branch, and to some extent, the Philadelphia branch, showed a large percentage of white European depositors," she said. "And the accounts for New York showed just how much money they came with. Some of them were depositing $200 or $400 as opposed to perhaps some of the formerly enslaved individuals who were living in the South."

"They did pull out their money first," says Yannelis, at the University of Chicago.

"They probably had better information than Black depositors for a lot of reasons. The headquarters of the bank was in New York, and later in D.C. So, at that time, news just travelled faster (in major cities). Also, due to the legacy of slavery, many Black deposit holders just didn't have education. So, they were less likely to do things like read a newspaper or be informed of the news."

Bank runs began. Large crowds begin to draw their money out of a bank because of a crisis, real or imaginary. Think of the photos of the start of Great Depression in the 1930s when depositors lined up outside banks nationwide.

But when the banks runs and the crisis started, the white depositors also were the first to leave. They started to leave 10 days to two weeks before the African American depositors.

"While some customers withdrew their savings, many others in the Black community kept their accounts. Business owners, pastors, teachers, churches and charities with strong local ties were left holding the bag, losing thousands of dollars when the bank collapsed," says J. Merritt Melancan in a University of Georgia article.

Wardlaw saw this as more than just lacking advance knowledge, but also called it "one of the great tragedies that the local communities of African Americans were just more invested in the mission of what was going on and didn't just want to bail on it, which is one of the more profound tragedies of the enterprise."

Chapter 7: It all comes crashing down

The vision that President Lincoln and the U.S. Congress had to provide a safe place for the formerly enslaved to place their sometimes-meager funds and to teach them about managing money began as a success. But, alas, it was eventually sabotaged by incompetence, corruption, an expensive and too-rapid expansion which the bank could not afford and a worldwide financial crisis.

Additionally, the assassination of Lincoln on April 14, 1865, led to the ascent into the presidency by Andrew Johnson, a former slaveowner and, arguably, one of the most racist presidents in U.S. history.

At first, things went well. With the Freedmen's Bureau helping to publicize it, the bank attracted millions of dollars from tens of thousands of depositors. The accounts they established were small – the majority of them between $5 and $50.

The Bank grew much too big, too fast

The bank was quick—perhaps too quick—to acquire the tangible symbols of success. It established branches throughout the country, which attracted new deposits but also depleted its resources.

Also, in 1867, the decision was made to move the bank's headquarters from New York to Washington, D.C., into a newly constructed splendid, but expensive, brownstone building. The new offices were built at the southeast corner of Lafayette Square, where the U.S. Treasury Annex stands today.

Frederick Douglass said that seeing the new headquarters filled his heart with pride:

"In passing it on the street I often peeped into its spacious windows and looked down the row of its gentlemanly and elegantly dressed colored clerks, with their pens behind their ears and button-hole bouquets in the coat fronts and felt very enriched. It was a sight I had never expected to see. I was amazed with the facility with which they counted the money. They threw off the thousands with the dexterity, if not the accuracy, of the old, experienced clerks.

"The whole thing was beautiful. I had read of this bank when I lived in Rochester and had indeed been solicited to become one of its trustees and had reluctantly consented to do so; but when I came to Washington and saw its magnificent brown stone front, its towering height, its perfect appointments, and the fine display it made in the transaction of its business, it was a sight I had never expected to see. I felt like the Queen of Sheba when she saw the riches of Solomon..."

But it had cost $260,000 to construct and furnish – a questionable expenditure for a bank that, within just a few years of its founding, was already experiencing problems.

Ebony Magazine's Lerone Bennett wrote in *The Shaping of Black America:*

"The view from the gallery was impressive; but behind the scenes things were going from bad to worse. Unbeknown to Douglass and other Black leaders, the bank had fallen into the hands of predators, who were making loans to one another and investing in overcapitalized and speculative ventures. According to later investigations, the bank was virtually controlled in its final years by the notorious New York financier, Jay Cooke. By 1872 the bank had been virtually destroyed by mismanagement and fraud."

Additionally, Congress' original intent was to create a bank in Washington, D.C., one without branches. Somehow, that intent was omitted from the final version of the legislation in the mad rush to pass the bill creating the bank. The Freedman's Bank ended up with 37 branches scattered across the Northeast, South, Southwest and Midwest. That made communication and oversight virtually impossible.

A nationwide network of bank branches was virtually unheard of at that time. In fact, most U.S. states banned interstate banking into the mid-1980s, and some, including New York state, even restricted statewide branch banking until the mid-1970s.

That system of branches took the bank to cities, large and small, that had large numbers of former slaves and/or large concentrations of Black Civil War troops. That rapid expansion would later haunt the bank and lead to its collapse. The communication problems were immense. That left the branches, which were led by inexperienced, and sometimes incompetent, staff with virtually no direction or oversight.

The bank grew fast – very fast – and had a huge network of branches, which was very unusual for the time. The geographic footprint was huge. Within seven years the bank collected $100 million (2021 dollars) from 100,000 Black depositors. [76]

The administrators of the Freedman's Bank had created a multi-state, multi-regional financial empire that was quite impressive. However, the bank was not prepared for the big problems that came with an operation of this magnitude.

Communication problems between the headquarters and the vast network of branches blew up into a big issue.

"Communications between the New York headquarters and the branches were poor at best; it took 11 to 12 days to receive a reply to a letter sent to New Orleans. Many branches in the Deep South had almost no contact with the central office. The sole inspector could not be everywhere at once; indeed, there were some branches that he never visited. Many amateurish cashiers ignored the tedious paperwork required by the central office. In 1866 Mahlon T. Hewitt, the bank's president, complained that only five branches regularly sent in reports."[77]

Local advisory boards were created to examine the financial transactions at the branches and certify each month that the cash and accounts were correct. But blossoming financial problems seemed to indicate that those boards were either negligent or incompetent, or both.

Created in 1863, just two years before the Freedman's Savings Bank, the Comptroller of the Currency (OCC) and his examiners were responsible for supervising the national banks it chartered, including several in the nation's capital. Under the national banking laws carried out by the OCC, real estate lending was explicitly forbidden—a prohibition enforced by the office's professional bank examiners.

Changing the bank's charter

When the bank moved to Washington in 1867, a group of local businessmen, bankers and politicians began to take control. The new trustees urged Congress to change the bank's charter. That's when the trustees started to invest in real estate and railroads. They also began to make risky loans to friends with no collateral. There were also trustees who were involved in other banks, and they transferred their bad loans to the Freedman's Bank.

By 1871, Congress had authorized the bank to provide mortgages and business loans. However, these mortgages and loans were given only to whites. That meant, ironically, the Freedman's Savings Bank was using the savings and pensions of its Black depositors to provide loans for whites who already had access to mainstream banks that excluded Blacks.

The bank's charter subjected it not to the authority of the OCC, but to Congress itself. By 1873, as the national economy spiraled downward, the bank's condition turned critical. Too late, Congress asked the OCC to assess its prospects, providing a special appropriation to conduct emergency examinations. The final nail in the coffin was the panic of 1873.

Part of the problem with the rapid expansion was that it was driven not by just business decisions, but by its missionary mission – the social goal of helping the freedmen learn not only about financial literacy, but to help them educate their children and survive.

The Postwar demobilization

A good part of the bank's financial crisis stemmed from the postwar demobilization of the Union troops – or more specifically the demobilization of the Black soldiers. After Appomattox, the Black regiments began to be discharged.

By April 1866 only one Black regiment remained in Georgia, two in Alabama and on each in South Carolina and Florida. By the end of 1867 the deposits that came from the soldiers' pay and back pay had, for the most part, ended.[78]

While it is not possible to estimate how much of the bank's deposits were from the Black soldiers, it is clear their deposits comprised the bulk of total deposits in the first few years of operation. But as U.S. began to draw down its army, the Black soldiers were leaving without jobs and with expenses of buying land and building homes. They needed their money.

Additionally, the families of the Black soldiers, some of them suffering, were anxious to get the male members of their families back home. And those homes, in many cases, were places where there was no Freedman's Bank branch.

The Panic of 1873

After the Civil War the U.S. banking system grew rapidly and seemed to be on solid ground, but the nation was plagued by numerous banking crises. One of the worst came in 1873 and proved to be the nail in the coffin for the Freedman's Bank.

The panic began in Europe, when the stock market crashed and investors began to sell off investments in American projects, especially railroads. Railroads were still fairly new, and companies used heavy borrowing to get the cash they needed to build new lines. Europeans began selling those railroad bonds, and soon they flooded the market and lost value. The railroads could no longer find cash investors, and many filed for bankruptcy.

Jay Cooke & Co., one of New York's largest banks, was in the middle of that bond debacle when it was discovered that the company had not placed as many of the bonds as it had led investors to believe, and they were, in fact, still on the bank's books. That meant Jay Cooke was sitting on a bunch of worthless assets.

"There was a run of the bank, and then run happened overnight," says Wardlaw, at the University of Georgia's Terry College of Business. "So, overnight, this thing goes insolvent, and then that sparks the panic of 1873 and depositors start to flee."

When Jay Cooke & Co. went bankrupt, people began runs on other banks. The panic spread to banks in Washington, D.C.,

Pennsylvania, New York, Virginia and Georgia, as well as others in the Midwest. At least 100 banks failed nationwide. And the impact on the Freedman's Savings Bank was undeniable.[79]

This collapse was disastrous for the nation's economy. A startling 89 of the country's 364 railroads crashed into bankruptcy. 18000 businesses failed over the next two years. Unemployment rose to 14 percent by 1876. The run on banks included the Freedman's Bank, but it didn't fold. However, deposits shrunk by three quarters from $4 million to $1 million because of withdrawals.

The Depression had a huge impact on southern Blacks – politically, socially and economically. Northern states, reeling from severe economic problems, no longer had the time to worry about the overt and pervasive racism in the South. White supremacist organizations such as the Ku Klux Klan, which had been somewhat suppressed during Reconstruction, resumed their campaigns of terror against the former slaves. By the time the nation began to emerge from the Depression, in 1879, those aligned with and sympathetic to the former slaveholders had regained power.[80]

Meanwhile, the Freedman's Bank's portfolio was decimated as the yield on government securities dropped precipitously. When the bank's board got the authorization to make real estate loans, those loans went to white investors in Washington, D.C., and they turned bad. Then, a white banker was able to trade toxic assets from his bank into the Freedman's Bank the results were disastrous.

Wardlaw says there are comparisons between the failure of the Freedman's Bank and the U.S. Savings and Loan Crisis in the 1980s, when the savings institutions started out making home loans, but then grew too fast and expanded into more risky areas.

That ultimately led to the failure of one third of the nation's 3,000 S&Ls between 1986 and 1995 at a total cost of $160 billion:

> "The sequencing of events, at least insofar as you can tell from the Congressional Records, is that that the (Freedman's Bank) is very successful in doing what it was initially chartered to do in the early days, when it had a handful of branches, in just taking in savings deposits and then, to try to pay interest on them. I think the board that ran it was a little sloppy. A lot of banks were sort of past sloppy at the time."

But the problems worsened, and the bank began taking actions that violated its charter.

The Trustees violate the charter – and ethics

In 1873 and 1874, OCC examiner Charles Meigs reported on the growing precariousness of the bank's position. In part because no one had been watching carefully over the bank's affairs, its officers had fallen victim to their own inexperience and to the machinations of the likes of Henry Cooke, who served on the bank's board while also serving his family banking business, using the assets of the former to benefit the latter.[81]

According to Brandon K. Winford, if you look at the Congressional testimony into the bank's failure, you see there was no accountability as the directors, like Cooke, took on loans that they did not repay.

In 1867 the bank's directors started using the deposits to make loans, clearly a violation of the bank's charter. But while 92 percent of the depositors were Black, 82 percent of the loans went to white borrowers, who were often part of the bank's elitist network. Almost all of those loans violated the bank's criteria for lending in its charter and more than 95 percent of the past due loans were not paid.[82]

When the bank moved to Washington in 1867, most of the original trustees resigned. Cooke, William S. Huntington and the actuary, D.L. Eaton took control of the bank's finance committee. That meant the loan approval committee was reduced to three.

Winford says the lack of accountability played a huge part in the bank's collapse.

> "You didn't have accountability, but you also didn't have a kind of checks and balance system assessing risks."

Several bank trustees who also sat on the boards of other financial institutions:

> "unloaded some of [their institutions'] bad loans on the Freedman's Bank. Others had relationships with companies that borrowed large sums, even though officials of the bank were prohibited by law from borrowing from it, directly or indirectly...There were not may officers after 1871 who was not connected with some outside company that borrowed from the bank."

An example of a conflict of interest – bank trustee Cook, a financier who had an interest in Jay Cooke and Co. and sat on the board of the Seneca Sandstone Co., pushed for the Seneca to receive an unsecured loan from the Freedman's Savings Bank. Seneca Sandstone defaulted on its loan, pushing the bank into bankruptcy.[83] "It just smells sort of corruption," says Wardlaw:

> "Regardless of whether the motives were well intentioned or dishonest and criminal, the result was the same: bank officers and trustees violated the charter in numerous unwise, unethical, and illegal actions which resulted in the loss of thousands of dollars belonging to the freedmen."[84]

Poor investments were made not only at the central office, but also at the branches. And the scandals were not confined to Washington. The Congressional investigations following the Freedman's Savings Bank's collapse uncovered dishonesty and incompetence among the cashiers. Some cashiers were charged with making illegal loans and others with outright theft.[85]

The bank kicked out Cooke and liquidated the portfolio of railroad bonds. But they continued to make real estate loans, mostly in Washington, D.C. It was profitable, the economy was booming, and it allowed the bank to pay a 6 percent rate to depositors. Wardlaw points out how far removed this is from the bank's original stated purpose:

> "But now you're sitting on an enterprise which is not what you promised the depositors. You are collecting money from (Black depositors in) New Orleans and Tennessee and Atlanta, and you are then funneling it into loans that you haven't really done a whole lot of due diligence on."

More than half of the loans were issued to real estate contractors, businessmen and financiers. The largest borrower, J. V. W. Vanderburgh, was the white owner of a construction firm working for the Board of Public Works of Washington, D.C. Theophile E. Roessle, the manager of Washington, D.C.'s most prestigious hotel, borrowed more than $78,000 in current dollars. In contrast, depositors of the bank were children or students (21 percent), cooks, washers, waiters or servants (13 percent), farm workers (13 percent), and construction workers (9 percent).[86]

Elected officials – senators, congressmen and state governors – received 15 percent of the loan volumes. For example, Maryland state senator Samuel Taylor Suit received a loan of $50,000 (current dollars). Public and real estate contractors received 41 percent of the loan volume. Railroad investors, such as Henry Cooke's brother, Jay Cooke, received 13 percent of the loan volume.[87]

Meanwhile, the bank rarely paid interest on deposits after 1872. The bank was, in effect, transferring money from its constituents (who had little or no access to capital) to friends, families and colleagues of the upper crust white trustees, like Jay Cooke.

In fact, the authors of the research paper, *Finance, Advertising and Fraud: The Rise and Fall of the Freedman's Savings Bank,* found that the vast majority of its loans violated the bank's charter. And borrowers strategically defaulted on their loans. Borrowers repaid only 5 percent of the loans due at maturity:

> "As a result, the bank, with no equity on its balance sheet, was insolvent from as early as 1872, long before the September 1873 panic. In January1873, the finance committee of the Freedman's Bank has already issued $3 million in loans which at least $900,000 were mature but not repaid. In the absence of equity, the bank was not only illiquid but also insolvent." [88]

Clearly, there was mismanagement at many branches, and that hurt the Freedman's Bank. Large sums of money were lost through faulty real estate loans. Douglass once wrote in a letter to abolitionist Gerit Smith that the Freedman's Bank was "The Black man's cow but the white man's milk."

Many of the Black depositors, both individuals and organizations, left their money in the bank. So, they felt the impact hard when failure came.

When the bank failed, 10 percent of the aggregate wealth of the targeted Black communities (those living within 50 miles of a bank branch) was due to depositors. In addition, more than 90 percent of the depositors identified in the 1870 census had zero or less than $100 in wealth. Congress agreed to repay depositors, but depositors recouped less than 20 percent of their deposits. [89]

Winford says the bank's failure had a huge impact on Black depositors because their funds on deposit were not so much for the future, but their deposits were from they needed for basic necessities.

> "Their survival was at stake, and so losing those funds threatened their very survival. It threatened the survival of their families. It threatened the survival of their communities. So, from an impact standpoint, we're talking about impacting their immediate survival."

Wardlaw, meanwhile, said one of the most striking occurrences was near the end – the last few months before the bank was shut down – you see an outflow of deposit by the bank's white depositors who were somewhere between 10 percent and 15 percent of the bank's customers.

> "You actually see that crater first, which is to say that they leave, and they managed to sort of pull their money out of the bank before the bank (collapsed)."

Many of those white customers were in New York, but they had deposits in other branches, also, Wardlaw said – attracted by a reasonably generous return on their deposits.

The verdict from W.E.B. Du Bois, while this was still within living memory, is that Black Americans lost far more than the money deposited with the bank:

> "Then in one sad day came the crash – all the hard-earned dollars of the freedmen disappeared; but that was the least of the loss – all the faith in saving went too, and much of the faith in men; and that was a loss that a Nation which to-day sneers at Negro shiftlessness has never yet made good.

> "Not even ten additional years of slavery could have done so much to throttle the thrift of the freedmen as the mismanagement and bankruptcy of the series of savings banks chartered by the Nation for their especial aid. Where

all the blame should rest, it is hard to say; whether the Bureau and the bank died chiefly by reason of the blows of its selfish friends or the dark machinations of its foes, perhaps even time will never reveal, for here lies un- written history."[90]

With 150 years of perspective, Rep Mfume says the bank gave the Freedmen hope, and then – in an instant - snatched it away.

"So, it hurt. It probably would have been better if there were no Freedmen's Bank to begin with. And I say it cautiously because it did help. But the hurt that came about as a result of it being snatched away from us, and being destroyed the way it was, created a pain that I think went on for a couple of generations after that."

In early 1874 the Freedman's Bank was on the brink of collapse, overwhelmed by the alterations to its charter that changed its loan and investment policy, the Panic of 1873, overexpansion, mismanagement, abuse, and outright fraud.

In March 1874, with the bank's existence threatened by the reports of corruption by the bank's white management, that management was replaced by prominent Blacks, most notably Frederick Douglass as president.

Douglass invested $10,000 of his own money to demonstrate his faith in its future. But after a few months of assessing the condition of the company, he realized that he was "married to a corpse" and recommended to Congress that the bank be closed.

Douglass's appointment was a move that many hoped would steady the bank in the eyes of its depositors, lest they withdraw their savings in a panic. But it was too late.

Congress, on June 20, 1874, authorized the trustees, with approval of the secretary of the treasury, to appoint a three-member board to take charge of the assets of the company and to report on its financial condition to the secretary of the treasury.

On June 29, 1874, less than a week after the act passed, the bank's trustees voted to shut it down, and the Freedman's Bank closed. In 1881 Congress abolished the board of three commissioners and authorized the secretary of the treasury to appoint the comptroller of the currency to oversee the affairs of the bank. The comptroller was required to submit annual reports to Congress. The final report of the comptroller was made in 1920.

During the Congressional hearings on the bank's collapse, the investigating committee recommended in 1876 that Henry Cooke and other directors be indicted.

> "...so gross a fraud and conspiracy to defraud, that, in the opinion of your committee, every one of the survivors of the transaction, viz, Henry D. Cooke, Lewis Clephane, Hallet Kilbourn and John O. Evans, should be indicted, tried and punished to the extent of the law."

However, ultimately, none of these men were held responsible. [91]

The closure of Freedman's Bank devastated the Black community. An idea that began as a well-meaning experiment in philanthropy had turned into an economic nightmare for tens of thousands African Americans who had entrusted their hard-earned money to the bank.[92]

Contrary to what many of its depositors were led to believe, the bank's assets were not protected by the federal government, resulting in the immediate loss of their tiny deposits. Perhaps more important was the deadening effect the bank's closure had on many of the depositors' hopes and dreams for a brighter future.

> "The bank's demise left bitter feelings of betrayal, abandonment, and distrust of the American banking system

that would remain in the African American community for many years. While half of the depositors eventually received about three-fifths of the value of their accounts, others received nothing."[93]

Considering that the majority of Blacks had only emerged from slavery less than a decade before, and that there were no government support programs, the impact on that population was quite significant, says Yannelis. Losing all their savings meant there was no money to send their children to school, but it also meant they could not even buy basic necessities.

It also helped to create a distrust of government institutions, says Vincent Brown, Charles Warren professor of American history and professor of African and African American studies at Harvard University. "So, people begin to feel betrayed by the Union, by the government in ways that are going to have lasting effects for generations."

The bank's collapse is one of the worst instances of depositor losses in the history of the U.S. banking industry. None of the other bank failures affected as many depositors. The bank's closing left 61,144 depositors with losses of nearly $3 million. It was years before some depositors received a portion of their savings. Many of the white depositors were reimbursed, but most of the smaller (Black) savers with passbook accounts received nothing.

Haskins said $10,000 invested back then, if you consider inflation, interest rates and other factors, could be worth several hundred thousand to $1 million. So, there is a direct relationship between those who lost money and the nation's persistent racial wealth gap.

Perhaps nothing summed up the debacle like Carl R. Osthaus at the end his book, *Freemen, Philanthropy, and Fraud,* considered by many historians and economists to be the definitive history of the Freedman's Savings Bank.

> "The collapse left a legacy of suspicion and failure which carried into the twentieth century. When (Booker T.) Washington and (W.E.B.) Du Bois and others spoke of Black economic enterprise, the legacy of the Freedman's Bank was still very real for Black Americans in many southern communities."

Du Bois wrote in his book *Black Reconstruction in America, 1860-1880*:

> "No more extraordinary and disreputable venture ever disgraced American business disguised as philanthropy than the Freedmen's Bank—a chapter in American history which most Americans naturally prefer to forget."

Black leaders knew even then that the devastation caused by the collapse of the bank would have long-term economic consequences for Black Americans – including a stubborn and persistent racial wealth gap that 150 years later still shows no signs of disappearing, or even narrowing.

Chapter 8: Long-term repercussions of the bank's failure: the racial wealth gap

Many historians, social scientists and economists cite the collapse of the Freedman's Bank as one of the defining moments in the creation of the nation's large and persistent racial Black-white wealth gap.

"There's a huge racial wealth gap in the United States that's persisted for a long time that we all want to close," said Yannelis at the University of Chicago's Booth School of Business. "Most of this gap is driven by the tragic history of the Black community in in the United States, but part of that is likely related to the experience of the Freedmen's Bank."

> "While it is widely known that there are severe disparities in wealth and income between black and white Americans, the origins of this are less appreciated. Indeed, before there was a Great Recession or a Great Depression, recently emancipated Black Americans had their first monies as freed persons mishandled and never returned in full."[94]

Within 10 years, this gift from President Lincoln turned into a setback that would last for generations to come. W.E.B. Du Bois said the failure of the Freedman's Bank did more damage to Blacks than an additional 10 years of slavery. The main lesson learned was not to trust the government:

> "Then in one sad day came the crash – all the hard-earned dollars of the freedmen disappeared; but that was the least of the loss – all the faith in saving went too, and much of the faith in men; and that was a loss that a Nation which today sneers at Negro shiftlessness has never been good."

The long-lasting ripple effect on Black Americans.

"It was a significant amount of money that folks lost when the Freedmen's bank collapsed," said Duke University's William A. Darity Jr. He estimates that the present value of the funds lost by Blacks when the bank collapsed, compounded at a conservative 4 percent interest rate, would be a total loss of $1.076 billion, or $17,946 per person. That's how much Black generational wealth was lost.

Darity describes the impact as an intergenerational problem of compounded exclusion and denial of opportunity:

> "It definitely had long term repercussions because it eliminated resources that could have been transferred to subsequent generations. So, it's the loss of resources across generations. That's the critical thing that comes into play from my point of view, and it was a significant amount of money that folks lost when the Freedmen's bank collapse."

Harold T. Epps, former Commerce Director for the City of Philadelphia, says every economic statistic shows that the disparities and gaps between Black and white Americans are profound and significant, and that "there's nothing to suggest that that disparities will be mitigated any time soon."

Today's statistics on the racial wealth gap:

- Although only 16 percent of Americans are "underbanked," today 27 percent of Blacks are underbanked. That means that they might have savings or checking accounts, but typically depend on alternative financial services like payday lenders, rent-to-own services, and check-cashing businesses.[95]
- The median wealth gap between the middle-class Black household and the middle-class white household in the U.S. is around $164,000. The average wealth gap is about $840,000.

Researchers at Rand found it would take $7.5 trillion to halve the wealth gap, and $15 trillion to eliminate it.[96]

- The homeownership rate for white Americans in 2021 was 72.7 percent, but the rate for Black Americans was 44 percent according to the National Association of Realtors. Also, people of color endure significant buying challenges throughout and even after their home purchase, according to the NAR.

- In every state across the U.S., Black households have lower homeownership rates than white households. That gap tends to be largest in states in the Northeast and Midwest. The gap between white households and households of color exceeded 30 percentage points in 13 states. For example, the widest gaps are in Connecticut (35.8 percentage points), South Dakota (35.7 percentage points), North Dakota (35.7 percentage points), and Wisconsin (35.4 percentage points). Gaps exceeded 30 percentage points in both relatively low-cost states like Iowa and Michigan, as well as higher-cost states like New York and Massachusetts.[97]

- White families have about six times more in average retirement savings than Black families, because workers with lower earnings have a harder time saving. The average white male earns $2.7 million over a lifetime, while the average Black male earns $1.8 million. Social Security is crucial for Black women, who typically live longer than Black men.[98]

- Between 2014 and 2018, nearly one in four Black women in the U.S. lived in poverty. Black mothers are only paid 50 cents of every dollar paid to white fathers. Black women are more likely than white women to be the primary breadwinners for their families, which impacts their ability to build wealth and savings.[99]

- Today, just 1 percent of farmers in the United States identify as Black according to the United States Department of Agriculture (USDA). These numbers are down from 1 million Black farmers a century ago. In 1919, Black farmland ownership peaked at 16 to 19 million acres, about 14 percent of total agricultural land. A century later, 90 percent of that land has been lost.[100]

- One potential source of the wealth gap is differences in the intergenerational transfer of wealth, either through bequests to heirs or through transfers among the living. The 1997 paper "Black-White Wealth Inequality: Is Inheritance the Reason?" estimated that inheritances account for 10 percent to 20 percent of the wealth gap. More recently, the 2020 paper "Can Income Differences Explain the Racial Wealth Gap? A Quantitative Analysis" indicated that intergenerational wealth transfers explain 26 percent of the gap.

- White-owned businesses have average annual sales of $439,579, compared with only $74,018 for Black-owned firms. Of the two million Black-owned businesses in the United States, fewer than 125,000 have employees. Only 7 percent have 6 to 10 employees, according to American Express research.

- One third of Black couples and two-thirds of unmarried Black seniors depend on Social Security for nearly all of their income.

- While older Black adults make up 9 percent of the older adult population, they represent 21 percent of that population living below the federal poverty level. The poverty rate for Black seniors is more than twice the rate of all seniors.

Black Americans lost half their wealth during the 2008 housing crash, and many have still not recovered. The Covid-19 pandemic crushed Black Americans even more. Some estimated that half of Black-owned businesses shut down during the pandemic.

Black wealth issues are not new problems. Rather, they are historically rooted in a persistent pattern of loss and mistreatment beginning with the mishandling of freedmen and freedwomen's money during Reconstruction.[101]

Black women and the racial wealth gap

Perhaps more than anyone else, Black women in the U.S. have been affected most by the nation's racial wealth inequities. For various reasons, Black women sit at the bottom rungs of the nation's economic system.

Black women are paid just 63 cents for every dollar paid to white American men. They are more likely impacted by both racial and gender discrimination, but also, they are more likely to work part time, have shorter careers and work in lower-paying industries. Also, Black women are more likely to go in and out of the job market, being the primary caregivers for their children and grandchildren. Black women are also more likely to be caregivers for other family members, including spouses and parents.

The median annual wage for Black women in the U.S. is $41,098 compared to $65,208 for white men.

The fact that they are underemployed and underpaid has an impact on their economic prosperity for life. That means they are less likely to have an employer-sponsored retirement plan, like a 401(k) or pension, and when they do, they are more likely to have a lower retirement balance.

Because they are not able to save, Black women in particular are more likely to be dependent on Social Security, which averaged $1,705 a month in 2023. Social Security payments are calculated based on career earnings. Black women spend less time in the job market and when they do work, they earn less, relegating them to a lifetime of retirement in poverty.

They are also more likely to outlive their spouses and are more likely to age with significant health issues. Black women are disproportionately affected by heart disease, stroke and diabetes, breast cancer, cervical cancer and fibroids.

Black women, Latinas, and Native Alaskan women are also disproportionately represented among women living in poverty. Black women represent 22.3 percent of women in poverty but make up only 12.8 percent of all women in the U.S. population.[102]

Tying it all to the Freedman's Bank

"What happened with the Freedman's bank literally is now our story," says Roland Martin, political analyst and CEO of Black Star Network:

> "We have never had a sustained period in this country where we were genuinely helped and assisted with being able to build and grow in America."

It's difficult to discuss the Freedman's Savings Bank and its ultimate collapse without discussing what could have been and what the impact could have been on the formerly enslaved and today's Black communities had it survived.

Wealth building

The failure of the Freedman's Savings Bank destroyed what could have been a strong financial foundation for Blacks in America. The impact of economic shocks is always long-lasting in Black communities, which are almost certain to be the last to recover. The housing crisis of 2008 and the COVID pandemic are the most recent examples of this.

Wealth doesn't build itself, says Haskins, the retired CEO of Harbor Bank in Baltimore, Maryland. Wealth is built through having access to capital, and that has been absent in Black America for decades, he says.

Liquidity

The families that trusted the Freedman's Bank with their savings would have had liquidity had it survived, said Michael Neal, principal research associate in the Housing Finance Policy Center at the Urban Institute. "If something bad would have happened, they would have been able to access their money to have to get through those difficult times. If you can't access your wealth, what's the point?"

More economic activity in the Black community

That economic activity would include homebuilding and small businesses, "You may as a young person start with your little transaction account," said Neal:

> "You get not just household financial benefits, but community benefits as well. More stable households lead to a more stable community, and that matters for home prices. That matters for you know, for the value of homes, not just that one person's home, but home values across the entire neighborhood."

Opportunities for an earlier increase of financial literacy

Neal says financial literacy comes by engaging with the financial system through a bank. Had the Freedman's Bank been a success, and had it remained in place for a long period of time, people would have had an understanding about how banks work and how to engage with them. And that financial acumen in these households would have been passed down to future generations.

He also says in the era of the Freedman's Savings Bank, the state of black wealth really was rooted in its potential. But in the end the bank's demise served to widen the racial wealth gap.

"...[I]t's not just that we jumped from the Civil War to redlining in the 1950's. We have these intervening experiences that systematically harmed the wealth accumulation of people of color."

In the book *Upswing, How America Came Together a Century Ago and How We Can Do It Again,* author Robert D. Putnam says life at the bottom of American society is improved, which leads some to say things will get better.

"But those gains have come mostly at the price of long hours in insecure low-wage work. Slavery has been abolished, of course, but the still ruthless reality of structural inequality condemns many people of color to a life of intergenerational poverty, and in some ways the situation of black Americans is actually worsening."

Black Americans have never had 25 years of "sustained economic growth" says Martin:

"...[T]hat is a fundamental problem... It's like we're in a war movie. (Gen. George) Patton said, 'I don't like having to fight for the same territory twice.' Well, that actually is the story of Black America. We literally are having to fight for the same territory over and over."

That lack of consistent economic growth in Black America has resulted in a plethora of related problems – from poverty, wage disparities, crime and violence, to low home ownership, growing health issues and health disparities.

Chapter 9: The long-term impact of racism on the health of Black Americans

You cannot have a discussion of racism and discrimination without talking about the impact the stress of racism has had on the health of Black Americans, especially older Black Americans. It might be a stretch to say the closing of the Freedman's Bank has resulted in this health crisis in Black America. But it is not a stretch to say the resulting debt crisis in Black America and the housing crisis and the history of discrimination by white banks have affected the physical and mental health of Black Americans.

According to the Centers for Disease Control and Prevention (CDC) a growing body of research shows that centuries of racism in the U.S. has had a profound and negative impact on communities of color:

> "The impact is pervasive and deeply embedded in our society – affecting where one lives, learns, works, worships and plays and creating inequities in access to a range of social and economic benefits – such as housing, education, wealth, and employment."

The report says these conditions are key drivers of health inequities in communities of color, putting those residents at greater risk for poor health outcomes. The data shows that racial and ethnic minorities in the United States have higher rates of health issues across a range of conditions, including diabetes, hypertension, obesity, asthma and heart disease when compared to their white counterparts.

The CDC says:

> "As a result, the life expectancy of non-Hispanic/Black Americans is four years lower than that of white Americans. The COVID-19 pandemic, and its disproportionate impact

among racial and ethnic minority populations is another stark example of these enduring health disparities."

Research recently published by Jennifer Hamil-Luker and Angela M. O'Rand indicates the current scale of household debt in the U.S., and how a disproportionate burden of that debt falls on Black Americans. The median debt-to-asset ratio is 50 percent higher among Black families compared to white families:

> "What this enormous debt burden means for people's health is unclear. A growing body of research links debt to poor health outcomes, such as depression, pain and poor self-reported health."[103]

Blacks are at higher risk for heart diseases, stroke, cancer, asthma, influenza and pneumonia, diabetes, and HIV/AIDS compared to white Americans, according to the U.S. Department of Health and Human Services' Office of Minority Health.[104]

Life expectancy has gradually increased over the last several decades for all Americans, says Dr. Keith B. Ferdinand, professor of medicine at the Tulane University School of Medicine.

> "But there's a persistent white-Black mortality gap… primarily driven by cardiovascular disease. That's heart disease and stroke. Black Americans have more hypertension, more uncontrolled hypertension and more complications of hypertension."

Four in 10 Black men aged 20 or older have high blood pressure, a rate 30 percent higher than that of white men. Black men's risk of a stroke is twice that of white men. For Black women, 45 percent of those aged 20 and older have high blood pressure, a rate 60 percent higher than white women.

- Black women are 40 percent more likely to die of breast cancer than white women.
- Black men have a 40 percent higher cancer death rate than white men.

- Black Americans are 80 percent more likely to be diagnosed with diabetes than whites, and nearly twice as likely to be hospitalized.
- Blacks are more than twice as likely as whites to suffer from Alzheimer's and other kinds of dementia.

Much of these health inequities can be attributed to systematic racism according to Dr. Celia Maxwell, Associate Dean of Research at the Howard University College of Medicine.

"Some of it might be attributed to genetics. But even with genetics, if you get consistently good care, you mitigate some of the bad outcomes. So...implicit bias and racism plays a role. You're getting sick with chronic illnesses earlier."

Debra Umberson, co-director of the Aging and Longevity Center at the University of Texas, Austin says that Black Americans face more lifetime stress than whites because of racial inequality and discrimination. They are also more likely to prematurely lose close family members, including children.

By the time Black Americans turn 60, they are 90 percent more likely than their white peers to experience at least four deaths of family.[105] Umberson says losing a child by the age of 40 increases the risk of developing dementia, which Blacks already face a higher risk of developing compared to whites.

Racism in hospitals

American history is filled with racist health care policies. Blacks were denied care at white-only hospitals, both public and private, for decades. There were some Black hospitals, mostly in major metropolitan areas, but the white hospitals that did admit Black patients relegated them to basement clinics.

Until the Civil Rights Movement in the 1960s Blacks were either denied access to hospitals or relegated to segregated wards. The first Black hospital, The Georgia Infirmary, was founded in 1832 and several others were created at the end of the 19th Century.[106]

For many Black Americans seeking emergency care, a white hospital might have been within five miles. Yet, the Black hospital was 60+ miles away. The white hospital would deny admission, forcing individuals to make the trek to the closest Black hospital, causing many to die trying to access proper care. This created a lasting stigma in Black America that loomed throughout the 1900s: "you only go to the hospital if you are dying."[107]

Most Americans don't realize that Medicare resulted in the desegregation of hospitals in the U.S. when it was enacted in 1965.

"Before the passage of Medicare and Medicaid, the U.S. health care system was segregated," said David Barton Smith, professor emeritus in healthcare management at Temple University in a U.S. News & World Report story, *Desegregation: The Hidden Legacy of Medicare.* Hospitals in the south complied with Jim Crow laws, excluding Blacks from hospitals reserved for whites or providing basement accommodations for them:

> "By threatening to withhold federal funding from any hospital that practiced racial discrimination, as required by Title VI of the Civil Rights Act of 1964, Medicare forced the desegregation of every hospital in America virtually overnight."

The 1918 flu epidemic

While Black Americans were less likely to get the flu, probably because they were less likely to interact with whites because of discrimination, they were more likely to die if they contracted it. The key reason being because of poverty, racism and isolation, Black Americans received substandard care in segregated hospitals—if they could even be admitted. Not many hospitals accepted Black Americans, and those that did sent them to the basement for care. There, they likely languished in rooms unintended for patient treatment, receiving neither the full resources nor timely medical attention white patients received in the main wards.[108]

A few Black hospitals existed at the time, including the Freedman's Hospital (now Howard University Hospital), in Washington, D.C., Provident Hospital in Chicago and Lincoln Hospital in New York City. Most Black people who did get sick with the flu ended up being treated in their homes by family members and midwives. Black doctors and especially Black nurses played a major role in caring for the Black community.

There are no accurate numbers on how many Black Americans who were infected or died in the pandemic because few Blacks had contact with health institutions. But worldwide more that 500 million people were affected, including 675,000 in the United States.

The Tuskegee experiment

Nothing captured the overt racism in the U.S. health care system like the so-called Tuskegee experiment. The U.S. Public Health Service and the Centers for Disease Control and Tuskegee Institute from 1932 to 1972 conducted a study of 400 unknowing Black men who were promised free medical care and thought they were being treated for syphilis. Instead, they were a part of a study on the effects of the disease if left untreated. More than 100 died.

When it was finally disclosed in 1972, the study ended, and the men sued. The result was a $9 million settlement and an apology from President Bill Clinton, 20 years later. In a White House speech, he said:

"The United States government did something that was wrong – deeply, profoundly, morally wrong. It was an outrage to our commitment to integrity and equality for all our citizens.

"To the survivors, to the wives and family members, the children and the grandchildren, I say what you know: No power on Earth can give you back the lives lost, the pain suffered, the years of internal torment and anguish."

The revelation of the experiment led to a distrust of health care and government agencies by Black Americans that still persists today. Some cited it as a major reason the Black community, especial in poorer neighborhoods, were resistant to the COVID-19 vaccines.

The CDC said in its National Immunization Survey:

"By the end of April 2021, when all U.S. adults were eligible to receive COVID-19 vaccine, vaccination coverage was highest among adults who were Asian (69.6 percent) or White (59.0 percent), and lower among those who were Hispanic (47.3 percent) or Black (46.3 percent),".

Later, those disparities narrowed, but they have not completely disappeared.

The COVID-19 pandemic

Nearly one-third of infections nationwide early in the pandemic affected Black Americans, according to the Centers for Disease Control, though Blacks represented only 13 percent of the U.S. population. Likewise, 25 percent of the deaths were Black.

Thirty-six percent of the pandemic deaths recorded in Wisconsin were among Blacks, though they comprise less than 7 percent of the state's population. 71 percent of fatalities in Shelby County,

Tennessee, which includes Memphis, were Blacks, who make up 50 percent of the population.

One of the reasons for the high infection and death rate in the Black communities was that Blacks historically have pre-existing health problems that made them more susceptible. Add to that poverty, lack of access to health care and the distrust of health care institutions, and the psychological strain of racism and discrimination.

The National Institute of Health (NIH) estimated that COVID reduced life expectancy for Black Americans by two years. According to the PNAS Journal (Proceedings of the National of Sciences of the United States):

"Estimated reductions for the Black and Latino populations are 3 to 4 times that for whites.

"Consequently, COVID-19 is expected to reverse over 10 years of progress made in closing the Black–White gap in life expectancy and reduce the previous Latino mortality advantage by over 70 percent."[109]

The pandemic also had an outsized impact on the Black community in other ways. Unemployment was higher. Blacks and other minorities were concentrated in the low-paying service jobs – hotels, restaurants especially – that were most severely affected by the pandemic shutdown.

Harold Epps, the former Philadelphia Commerce Director, says the pandemic deaths in the Black community will affect those households for generations to come. The deaths will affect earning potential, and even deny some children the opportunity to go to college. He concludes that "as a result, the wealth gap has widened. The educational gap has widened. And those things are generational."

The impact was doubly had on top of the losses suffered by Blacks in what they failed to recoup after the 2008 global financial crisis.

Ferdinand, professor of medicine at the Tulane University School of Medicine says that because of the isolation during COVID, many people weren't able to maintain control of their medical conditions, especially those with multiple risk factors including hypertension, diabetes and heart disease. That actually increased the white-Black mortality gap, he says.

Violence and homicides in the Black community

Violent crime has been increasing in cities across America since the COVID-19 pandemic. That violent crime is widely considered to be a racial health disparity issue.

Some communities and groups are far more exposed to the poor neighborhood conditions that give rise to violence and other health inequities, according to a fact sheet from the Prevention Institute. "Poverty, racism, and lack of educational and economic opportunities are among the fundamental determinants of poor health and lack of safety."

According to federal crime statistics, people 18 to 21 are the most likely to experience a serious violent crime, and Blacks in that age group were the most vulnerable: 72 victimizations per 1,000 blacks vs. 46 victimizations per 1,000 for whites.

In 2022, the murder rate among Blacks is 653 percent higher than the murder rate for whites, according to the Crime Prevention Research Center. The murder rate for Hispanics is 65 percent higher than for whites. From 1990 through 2022, the Black murder rate averaged 569 percent higher than whites.
The Journal of the National Medical Association, representing Black doctors and health professions, says it is impossible to have

a conversation about health equity without speaking about violence. Despite a decline in overall rates in the United States since 1999, there has been a significant increase in homicides in the Black communities. "Gang Violence, Intimate Partner Violence (IPV) and Child Maltreatment as well as Police Use of Excessive Force are major subsets of violence that disparately and disproportionately affect communities of color," the Journal says.

It's not much of a reach to connect the gun violence in Black community to factors like historical segregation, poverty and discrimination – all of which could have been improved to some extent had the Blacks had not lost millions in the collapse of the Freedman's Bank.

A study by Wharton School professor of statistics, Dylan Small, says gun violence is four times higher in neighborhoods with mostly Black residents vs. neighborhoods with mostly white residents. One reason, he said, is that Black families have systematically lower household wealth than white families, including lower home values.

Clearly, the health and wealth inequities in Black communities are related, especially in poor Black communities. Probably most concerning is that there will not be any improvement long-term health issues and inequities until the racial wealth gap is narrowed or eliminated.

Chapter 10: Black Americans and poverty

Blacks make up 13.5 percent of the U.S. population, yet they account for slightly more than 20 percent of the nation's population living in poverty, according to the U.S. Census Bureau.

The number is considerably worse in major cities. For example, in Washington, D.C., the nation's capital, Black residents are five times more likely to live in poverty and have one-third the income of white residents. Those numbers were impacted by the COVID pandemic, which pushed the percentage of Blacks in poverty up to 27.7 percent in 2021, from 21.6 percent in 2019, census data shows.

In Chicago, Illinois, the majority Black South Side and West Side had the highest concentration of poverty. "Extremely high poverty rates in dense minority neighborhoods is a large reason why citywide, Black Chicagoans face poverty at a rate of 28.7 percent. That's nearly *triple* what white Chicagoans experience at 10.3 percent," says a report from the Illinois Center for Poverty Solutions.

Poverty rates for Black families vary based on the family type. According to Black Demographics, a resource for information on Black Americans, while just under 19 percent of all Black families live below the poverty level only 7 percent of Black married couple families live in poverty.

> "That's considerably lower than the 31 percent of Black families headed by single women who live below in poverty. The highest poverty rates (39 percent) are for Black families with children which are headed by single Black women. This is significant considering more than half (55 percent) of all Black families with children are headed by single women."

Those stubbornly high poverty rates among Blacks, especially Black women, can be traced back to years of racial discrimination in housing, education, health, employment and the American justice system.

KFF, an independent source of health policy research reports exorbitantly high Black poverty rates across the U.S:

10 states with high Black poverty rates

	White	Black
Alabama	11.6 percent	26.8 percent
Arkansas	13.8 percent	29.5 percent
Idaho	9.0 percent	28.2 percent
Illinois	8.4 percent	25.6 percent
Indiana	10.3 percent	25.0 percent
Iowa	9.3 percent	37.5 percent
Louisiana	12.9 percent	29.1 percent
Maine	9.5 percent	31.6 percent
West Virginia	17.0 percent	32.6 percent
Wyoming	11.1 percent	37.0 percent

"Black people's inability to build meaningful wealth has its roots in the very inception of this nation," says the report, *Homelessness and Black History: Poverty and Income,* by the National Alliance to End Homelessness (NAEH):

"While on its face, the end of slavery should have meant the opportunity for Black people to build wealth, in reality each generation of Black Americans since the end of slavery has faced a new, even more insidious set of obstacles to obtaining and keeping wealth, status, and stability.

"The abolition of outright slavery in the U.S. quickly led to the introductions of even more insidious barriers to equity, including sharecropping, forced prison labor, Jim Crow segregation laws, and voter disenfranchisement. These new institutions made life very difficult for Black people in the nineteenth and twentieth centuries and made wealth accumulation nearly impossible."[110]

After U.S. cities across the nation erupted in race riots in the mid- to late-1960s President Lyndon Johnson appointed the Kerner Commission, which in its 1968 report found that racism, not Black anger, was the root of the problem:

"Segregation and poverty have created in the racial ghetto a destructive environment totally unknown to most white Americans. What white Americans never fully understood – but what the Negro can never forget – is that white society is deeply implicated in the ghetto. White institutions created it, white institutions maintain it, and white society condones it."[111]

The Kerner Commission warned that the nation was so divided that the United States was poised to fracture into two radically unequal societies—one black, one white.

Fifty years later the Black Lives Matter protests following the murder of George Floyd by a white policeman led to similar determinations, though the focus this time turned mostly to the police and the American justice system.

"While Floyd's death changed the world at large, the tragedy was a stark reminder, specifically for Black Americans, of the deep systemic realities underlying Black life," said a report by NBC News.

Poor Black Americans are mired in a generational cycle of misery and despair. Poverty rates are higher for adults who were poor during childhood.

William A. Darity Jr. and A. Kirsten Mullen, authors of *From Here to Equality: Reparations for Black Americans in the Twenty-First Century,* said Black Americans constitute 13 percent of the nation's population but only possess about 2 percent of the nation's wealth. That corresponds to an $850,000 deficit between the average Black and white household in terms of mean wealth.

The reasons for the high poverty rates in Black communities are pretty much the same as they are for most of the racial inequities in the country – racism and discrimination in employment, housing and the American system of justice. In fact, the group Prosperity Now predicts that the average net worth of Black Americans will average zero by 2053.

Jobs and employment

Despite an improved labor market, Black Americans still can't obtain well-paying, stable jobs with quality benefits, according to the Center for American Progress:

> "There are several factors that have contributed and continue to contribute to this. These include repeated violent oppression of African Americans such as the riots that destroyed Black business owners' wealth on the Black Wall Street in Tulsa, Oklahoma in 1921, codified segregation, legal racial terrorism during the almost century long period from Reconstruction to the civil rights era, systematic exclusions of African Americans from better-paying jobs and continued occupational segregation."[112]

Statistics from the U.S. Bureau of Labor Statistics show that historically, unemployment among Black men and women has been double that of white Americans since 1972. Their findings show that Black teens, Black women and Black men's unemployment in the United States is consistently worse that of white teens, white women and white men.

From 1972 to 2004 the average rate of unemployment was 12.4 percent for black males versus 5.4 percent for whites. The unemployment rate among Black teens reached a high of 36 percent in 2020 but was down to 24 percent in the third quarter of 2023.

Blacks' unemployment rates are also considerably higher during economic shocks, like the Great Recession of 2008 and the COVID-19 pandemic.

- Unemployment for Blacks reached nearly 9 percent during the 2008 recession vs. 6.3 percent for whites. "Minorities were at least more than 40 percent more likely than whites to experience unemployment at the end of 2008," said The Center for American Progress. "Here we are, years later, and we still haven't recovered," said Black Star Network CEO, political commentator and author Roland Martin.
- Black unemployment peaked at 16.8 percent in 2020 during the height of the Covid pandemic, according to the White House.
- In 1933, during the Depression, Black unemployment reached 50 percent, according to the Library of Congress. The unemployment rate for the nation peaked at 25 percent.

Blacks are also concentrated in low paying service jobs. They make up 12 percent of the American workforce but accounted for 36 percent of those working as security guards and 36 percent of nursing and home health aides. Black workers made up 12 percent of low-wage entry level jobs, vs. 7 percent of managerial jobs, says a report from McKinsey. And the Economic Policy Institute says that in 2019 the typical Black worker earned nearly 25 percent less than the typical white worker.

According to a 2020 report from Citi, *Closing the Inequality Gap*, if the Black wage, education, housing and investing gaps had been closed 20 years ago, it would have added an estimated $16 trillion to the U.S. economy, with the Black pay gap alone accounting for $2.7 trillion.

These inequities in the current economic system still haunt Blacks because they earn from 14 percent to 30 percent less on average than their counterparts, says Eric Bailey, a certified financial planner (CFP) and founder of Bailey Wealth Advisors in Silver Spring, Maryland.

> "It exacerbates the problem because we have less disposable income during our working years. Without discretionary income, it becomes difficult for people to save and accumulate wealth."

Homeownership

Homeownership rates among Black households stand at 44 percent vs. 73 percent for whites. The gap between white and Black homeownership rates is wider now than it was in 1960, when housing discrimination was rampant and legal. Black homeownership has declined in every state in the past decade.

Black Americans are less likely to have wealthy, homeowning parents, as the National Alliance to End Homelessness report says. Research shows that having wealthier parents correlates strongly with economic stability later in life. Having homeowning parents increases the likelihood that a child will eventually go on to become a homeowner themselves. Historical forms of racism like housing discrimination mean that the parents and grandparents of Black people living today are far less likely to have owned homes than white members of their cohort.

> "This means that where white people are more likely to benefit from generational cycles of wealth and ownership, Black people are less likely to go on to have wealth, own homes, or have stable housing. Because homeownership is

a key strategy for accumulating wealth, these conditions even further entrench racial wealth disparities."[113]

Children in poverty

According to the Children's Defense Fund historical, systemic racism and institutional barriers have left children of color particularly vulnerable to child poverty.

"Black and Hispanic children experience some of the highest poverty rates in the country, and 71 percent of children in poverty in 2019 were children of color. More than 1 in 5 children of color in America (20.5 percent) were poor. Children of color were 2.5 times more likely to be poor than their white, non-Hispanic peers."

Though progress has been made in the fight against child poverty over the past several decades, due in large part to government policies, there has been little headway made in narrowing the Black-white child poverty gap, according to the Center on Poverty and Social Policy at Columbia University. Black children were more than three times as likely to live in poverty than white children.

Aging in poverty

The Economic Policy Institute says the majority of elderly Blacks (63.5 percent) are "economically vulnerable." The author of the report states:

"After working hard their entire lives, millions of our elderly are struggling to pay for basic needs like food, medicine and housing, even with Social Security and Medicare."

KFF said that according to the U.S. Census Bureau, the poverty rate is substantially higher among Black and Hispanic adults aged 65 and older than among white adults in the same age group, particularly for Black and Hispanic women. Additionally, more than 60 percent of older Black and Hispanic women have incomes below 200 percent of poverty compared to 41.4 percent of white women.

Older Black Americans have a huge dependency on Social Security. According to the U.S. Social Security Administration, about 38 percent of minority beneficiaries rely on Social Security for 90 percent or more of their income compared with 28 percent of whites. The average monthly Social Security check is only $1,700.

The justice system

It has been estimated that nearly 28.5 percent of Black males are likely to be imprisoned. According to the U.S. Department of Justice Office of Justice Programs a Black male today has a greater than 1 in 4 chance of going to prison in his lifetime. Cunningham, the former Prosperity Now CEO states:

> "So, say you got a third of the black male population incarcerated. If you're 18 to the 24 or 25 there are more of us in prison than there are in college."

The social justice protests in the U.S. in 2020, which spread around the world, pointed to racism and discrimination among police in the killing and arrests of Black men and women. The protests were prompted by the killings of unarmed Black men and women, most notably George Floyd. Several of the officers involved in those killings were later arrested and convicted.

The rise of the Black Lives Matter movement following the 2014 shooting of Michael Brown, an unarmed Black man, in Ferguson, Missouri, focused attention on how police and officials in municipalities across the United States used traffic stops and fines imposed on Black communities to fund city budgets, according to

The London School of Economics. That research found that cities with larger Black populations collect a greater number of fines.

The trauma of violence in poor Black communities

In many communities of color, homicide is one of the leading causes of death. "This type of violence has a 'ripple effect', adversely affecting a community's ability to gain equitable access to education, economics, housing and health care," according to *The Violence Epidemic in the African American Community: A Call by The Medical Association for Comprehensive Reform.*

Harold Epps says the trauma, from the shock of violence at an early age stays with young kids for life, and it also affects future generations:

> "That changes your whole relationship with society forever. The trauma we are seeing in our African American experience in this country over 400 years leaves us significantly behind our white counterparts per capita in every dimension."

Public assistance

According to the U.S. Census Bureau, 14.5 percent of Black Americans receive housing assistance, including government housing or section 8 housing, according to Black Demographics. Also, 2.5 percent receive Temporary Assistance for Needy Families (TANF) cash assistance, formerly referred to as welfare. The largest benefits received by African Americans include the 29 percent receiving Medicaid health insurance and 30 percent of African Americans who receive SNAP Food Stamps. About 42 percent of Black Americans (mostly children) received some sort of public assistance.

While pervasive poverty remains one of the big issues that we still attribute to the closing of the Freedman's Savings Bank in 1874, there are, of course, there are many related issues. One of the most impactful is the distrust of banks and financial institutions, especially among poor Blacks.

The Urban Institute sums it up in a 2023 report, *Building Trust in the Financial System Is Key to Closing The Wealth Gap*:

> "Given the history of banking in the United States—which was created when slavery was still legal, deliberately excluded Black Americans for a century, and then employed discriminatory practices such as redlining and subprime lending—it is not surprising that many Black Americans are hesitant to engage with banks."

Chapter 11: The Bank's collapse still impacts Black America's relationship with banking – 150 years later

Black America's relationship with the banking and finance industry has a long and complicated history. Their first real relationship was with the Freedman's Savings Bank – and we know how badly that ended.

But that ugly chapter in history was followed by years of discrimination and outright hostility.

Black Americans are less likely to use banks and financial services than other groups in this in the United States. And then when you ask them why they're not using banks, the answer that people give mostly is that they lack trust in the banking system.

Constantine Yannelis of the University of Chicago Booth School of Business says he found a direct correlation between the failure of the Freedman's Bank and that deep distrust of banks - more than 150 years later.

The Freedman's Bank's failure was certainly a tremendous blow. Many of the poorest individuals lost every penny they had saved.

Black Americans had taken pride in the Freedman's Bank. At a time when some people were saying that ex-slaves could not make it on their own, the Freedman's Bank was one piece of demonstrable proof that they could. Ministers, community leaders, and teachers had worked hard to convince people to trust the bank.

Yanellis states that even to this day, individuals living closer to Freedmen's bank branches are less likely to trust financial institutions.

A big loss, especially for poor Black people

Blacks lost $3 million in deposits when the bank collapsed, which would be $69 million in today's dollars. "But whether it's $3 million or it's $69 million, that's a big loss for a lot of people and a lot of investors who could not do very much about it," said Rep. Mfume.

Considering how low the incomes were of the Black veterans and Freedmen, Prof. Darity says, whatever funds they had in the banks would have been, for them, significant. Given that, he said, there would be an obvious reluctance to deal with the banking system after that. "When people get screwed, they're going to be less inclined to (open) bank accounts," he says.

Yannelis points out that because of extreme racism and segregation in the south, for most Black people, it was their only experience with a bank:

> "Other banks would not serve Black customers due to the fact that most of the population came out of slavery less than a decade before. They don't have any experience with financial institutions. So, in these communities the only experience that people have with finance and banks is just an unmitigated catastrophe. You see a large fraction of the people losing their life savings so that the whole community is devastated."

Congress authorized that those who lost money in the bank's collapse receive 62 cents on the dollar. But that did not mean most of the depositors ever collected that money.

Mfume commented:

> "Most people who were due the money, never got it. So, it left a very, very bitter taste in the mouths of a number of Black citizens who were trying to do the right thing. They

worked hard they played by the rules. They loved their country. They cherished their faith, and they invested their dollars. However, in this investment, they got burned and burned really bad."

Mfume said though there was not a lot of news coverage on the bank's failure at that time, but there was word of mouth among the Black community. It permeated the memories of those in the Black community. As a result, Blacks started finding alternatives to saving their money – putting it in a sock or hiding it under a mattress – "whatever they had to do to protect it that would allow them access to it."

Despite their vastly different views and philosophies on socialization and politics, both W.E.B. Du Bois and Booker T. Washington agreed that the collapse of the Freedman's Savings Bank was a devastating blow to the confidence and livelihood of the scores of Black depositors who had trusted the bank with their savings.

Washington, founder of Tuskegee Institute and one of the nation's most influential Black leaders of the 19th and late 20th Centuries wrote:

> "When they found out that they had lost, or been swindled out of all their savings, they lost faith in savings banks, and it was a long time after this before it was possible to mention a savings bank for Negroes without some reference being made to the disaster of [the Freedmen's Bank]."

Du Bois, writing later in *The Souls of Black Folk*, said the impact was huge and long lasting:

> "Not even ten additional years of slavery could have done so much to throttle the thrift of the freedmen as the mismanagement and bankruptcy of the series of savings banks chartered by the Nation for their especial aid."

The loss of those funds was devastating because the funds were no longer available to working people to buy homes, seeds for crops or other daily necessities.

Yannelis said the Freedman's Bank was a huge historical experience because it had such a large footprint in Black communities in the South.

"One in seven Black people throughout the South lived in families that had a branch nearby,

"Everybody knows somebody. If they're not personally impacted, they know somebody who has just lost their life savings, they've had a major wealth shock, and this is a particularly vulnerable community."

According to Michael Neal, at the Housing Finance Policy Center at the Urban Institute in Washington, D.C., that bitter ending for Freedmen's Bank contributed to what was already an eroding trust, eroding credibility, in the banking sector, maybe even in the financial industry, more generally. For years after the failure of the bank, Blacks were excluded from the banking sector, adding to the distrust.

Among the inequities many Black and LatinX consumers in the U.S. face, one of the most concerning is the lack of access to necessary financial products and services. Making up just 32 percent of the US population, Black and LatinX households represent 64 percent of the country's unbanked and 47 percent of its underbanked households.[114]

According to a Federal Deposit Insurance Corporation (FDIC) 2021 survey of unbanked and underbanked households, 4.5 percent of U.S. households were unbanked. The rates were higher for lower-income households, less educated households, Black households, Hispanic households, working age households with disabilities and single mother households. Nearly 14 percent of

Black households did not have a checking or savings account at a bank or credit union.

Differences in unbanked rates between Black and white households in 2021 were present at every income level, the report said. For example, among households with income between $30,000 and $50,000, 8 percent of Black households were unbanked compared with 1.7 percent of white households.[115] The top reasons for being unbanked were not enough funds to meet minimum balance requirements (22 percent) and "don't trust banks" (13.2 percent).

A lack of access to these mainstream banking systems, which are the foundation for wealth building, has led Black people to have significantly lower net worth and homeownership rates than their white counterparts, on average, at every stage of their lives, said to the Urban Institute.

Neal said though the Freedman's Bank had good intentions as a "Black bank" set up to bring Black people into the financial system and be supportive of them as they navigate the system, over time, the change in focus towards whites contributed to the eroding trust.

Perhaps more relevant is the treatment of Blacks by banks in the 150 years since the Freedman's Bank closed. The history of the treatment of Blacks in the finance history has not been good.

Haskins, for example, said banking for Black Americans was not an open-door welcoming environment. That, he said, is one reason there was a need to form Black institutions:

> "Even though there were those who were willing to still trust banking, some were denied opportunities because majority banks, for the longest period of time did not

welcome African Americans . And we can see that occurring all the way up to about the 1940s".

Neal was one of the authors of the Urban Institute report, *Building Trust in the Financial System is Key to Closing the Wealth Gap*, which said for the financial system to be equitable and sustainable, banks must do more to gain Black Americans' trust.[116]

That report said banks need partnerships with minority depository institutions; and continue to seek relationships with churches and other nonprofits working to support Black neighborhoods; prioritize greater staff diversity at all levels; and collect data to determine what works and where more effort is needed.

Neal said the suspicion and lack of trust in banks prevalent among some in the Black community has had an impact on the racial wealth gap in several ways: less access to the financial services used to attain wealth and higher rates and harsher terms for products and services.

"When you have redlining, racially restrictive covenants, you have other tools of discrimination remaining in place, then in some ways, those potential benefits remain a bit limited. If we had used them, we would have built more wealth. To a degree that's limited because of the other pervasive things that were going on."

It's a shame in many ways because, by and large, financial services are a major way to wealth accumulation. Acquiring savings and property are the way to acquire wealth. And if you take advantage of financial services, you won't eliminate the majority of the racial wealth gap, but you might eliminate some of it.

For Americans, most of their wealth is in their homes. But it's hard to acquire a home without a bank account. As Yannelis says,

"It's just very difficult to accumulate enough cash. And it's also very risky. If there's a fire, your home burns down or if somebody breaks in and steals large amounts of cash and you don't have a bank account."

Epps, the former Philadelphia director of commerce, meanwhile, compared the collapse of the Freedman's Bank to the Tuskegee syphilis study (see page 90 above), conducted between 1932 and 1972:

"That left us with a level of distrust. We wouldn't take a COVID shot that all the medical studies said was going to save your life, because we still had distrust of the government's intervention in healthcare 100 years ago."

He said historically, Black people were putting their money under the mattress when whites were putting their money in banks:

"Wealth lost is wealth opportunity deprived,

"In many cases, even today, many African Americans still don't keep all of their money in banks. And when they do put most of their money in banks, often, they spread it out between several banks, so it's not concentrated. Because if one fails, you're not totally deprived of all of your resources."

That complicated relationship with banks also hurts the community's access to housing wealth. Banks and white real estate agents discriminated against people of color for years with discrimination was unwritten, but there were laws and rules that were also written into law. And though those laws may not be thoroughly enforced today, some of them remain on the books in state and municipal laws and in housing covenants in communities across the nation.

Chapter 12: The Freedman's Bank and the impact on Black housing wealth

In an earlier chapter Duke University economist and author William A. Darity estimated that the present value of the funds lost by Blacks when the Freedman's Savings Bank collapsed, compounded at a conservative 4 percent interest rate, would be a total loss of $1.076 billion, or $17,946 per person. That's just one indication of how much Black generational wealth was lost in the Freedman's Bank debacle.

That $3 million ($69 million in today's dollars) lost by Black Civil War veterans, former slaves and free Blacks in 1874 wiped away what could have been a century and a half of generational wealth – money that could have potentially been used to help Blacks buy homes and property that they could leave to their children, grandchildren and future generations.

Since the bank's 37 branches spread deep into the South, to the North and Midwest, the impact was, at that time, huge. Blacks at that time were concentrated in the North and South United States.

Today, home ownership is the largest source of wealth among families in the United States. The median value of a primary home is worth about 10 times the median value of other financial assets held by families, according to the Federal Reserve.

But home ownership rates among Black households stands at 44 percent vs. 73 percent for whites. A study by Rugh says that Black homeownership has dropped to the lowest levels since the 1968 Fair Housing Act. In fact, that gap between white and Black homeownership rates is wider now than it was in 1960, when housing discrimination was both rampant and legal. Black homeownership has declined in every state in the past decade.

The result is a growing racial homeownership disparity between the share of Black families that own homes and the share of white families that own homes of 29 percent, up from 26 percent in 2011.

Also, homeowners had a median net worth of $255,000 – more than 40 times the median net worth of renters, which is $6,300.

In fact, a study by Citigroup said that not addressing racial gaps between Blacks and whites has cost the U.S. economy $16 trillion over the last two decades alone. According to them:

> "Improving access to housing credit might have added an additional 770,000 Black homeowners and added $218 billion in sales and expenditures."

Though the shutdown of the Freedman's Bank was a contributor to many aspects of the racial wealth divide, the Black home ownership crisis is the result of many factors – chief among them racism and discrimination.

Black Star Network CEO and political commentator Martin said:

> "We get the highest point of home ownership under President Bill Clinton, then – boom – the 2007-2008 home foreclosure crisis hits and 53 percent of Black wealth is wiped out,

> "It will be 100 years to recoup what we lost in 2008."

Angry white mobs and race riots

Nick Abrams, a Certified Financial Planner in Hunt Valley, Maryland notes:

> "If we look back historically, going back to the Black Wall Street era (the prosperous section of Black Tulsa, Oklahoma before it was burned to the ground by whites), anytime we started accumulating some type of wealth, especially

coming out of the era of slavery and going into reconstruction, those towns and those businesses were decimated,

"And we had to start over and over again, which has limited our ability to create that generational wealth."

Massacres and riots destroying Black wealth, Black businesses and Black lives happened in dozens of American cities, before and after the Tulsa, Oklahoma massacre. These riots occurred in cities ranging from Chicago, Detroit, New York, Washington, D.C., Wilmington, Delaware and Atlanta.

This rampant and violent destruction of Black lives and property plagued by these angry mobs happened in the 19th Century in cities like Thibodaux, Opelousas, and Colefax, New Orleans and St. Bernard Parish, Louisiana, Vicksburg and Clinton, Mississippi, and Eufaula and Camilla, Georgia.

Black Tulsa residents filed claims for $1.8 million (all of which were denied), which would be $27 million in today's dollars. A 2018 article in the American Journal of Economics and Sociology on the impact of the Tulsa massacre said:

"If 1,200 median priced houses in Tulsa were destroyed today, the loss would be about $150 million. The additional loss of other assets including cash, personal belongings and commercial property, might bring the total to $200 million."

Blacks have had their property lost, destroyed or stolen at every juncture in American history, says Martin.

"How many Black people literally left land and property because they were being threatened with being killed? And so, our entire history has been starts and stops."

In Philadelphia more than 200 Black families attempting to rent or buy in the city's segregated communities were attacked in the first six months of 1955 alone.[117] In Los Angeles Blacks faced violence when they tried to move from segregated communities between 1950 and 1965. The attacks included dynamite bombings, cross burnings, and rocks thrown through windows. Those attacks led to only one arrest.

Philadelphia's Epps states:

> "Systems institutions and people have taken property that was not theirs and made it theirs every which way you can imagine – falsifying tax records, shooting you, killing you, falsifying paperwork,

> "You name it it's been done. And one (race) has built generational wealth and the others have had generational disenfranchisement, which has meant now we have one with generational poverty."

Redlining

One major contributor to the Black-white racial wealth divide is the systemic policy support for white homeownership and systematic barring of Black homeownership through federal policies that created redlining and the modern mortgage market in the 1930s.

Richard Rothstein, a distinguished fellow at The Economic Policy Institute, in his book *The Color of Law*, said the root of the racial wealth gap lies in systematic, legalized housing discrimination over three decades – starting in the 1940s – that prevented Black families from having a piece of the American Dream of home ownership.

Black families that were prohibited from buying homes in the suburbs in the 1940s and 50s and even into the 1960s by the Federal Housing Administration gained none of the equity appreciation that whites gained, Rothstein said.

The discrimination happened on several levels – and often culminated in violence against Black families trying to move into neighborhoods that had been effectively designated as white by government policy. Sometimes those designations took place quite literally as maps were divided up along racial lines with different colors on maps. Black neighborhoods were painted red – hence the term redlining – which only became illegal after the Fair Housing Act of 1968.[118]

The U.S. Commission on Civil Rights, in its 1959 report said called housing "the one commodity in the American Market that is not freely available on equal terms to everyone who can afford to pay." Two years later, the 1961 United States Commission Civil Rights Report, said "the situation is not much better."

> "Throughout the country large groups of American citizens – mainly Negroes, but other minorities too – are denied an equal opportunity to choose where they will live. Much of the housing market is closed to them for reasons unrelated to their personal wealth or ability to pay. New housing, by and large, is available only to whites. And in the restricted market that is open to them, Negroes generally must pay more for equivalent housing than do the favored majority."[119]

The report said there was plenty of blame to go around for housing discrimination.

> "A number of forces combine to prevent equality of opportunity in housing. They begin with the prejudice of private persons, but they involve large segments of the organized business world. In addition, Government on all levels bears a measure of responsibility – for it supports and indeed to a great extent it created the machinery through which housing discrimination operates."

Redlining was a major contributor to homes in Black communities appreciating at a much lower rate than in white communities, Epps says.

> "We have generations of verification that the appreciation rate is outrageously different within a five-mile radius, based upon redlining and who will live there,
>
> "And all that comes out in the same system of abuse, distrust and racism by decision makers who 99 times out of 100 were white."

According to a Washington Post article, "racial discrimination in mortgage lending in the 1930s still shapes the demographic and wealth patterns." A National Community Reinvestment Coalition study found that 3 out of 4 neighborhoods "redlined" on government maps 80 years ago continuing to struggle economically.

The 2019 study showed that most neighborhoods marked "hazardous" in red ink on maps drawn by the federal Home Owners' Loan Corp. from 1935 to 1939 are today much more likely than other areas to comprise of lower-income, minority residents.

There were Black banks scattered across the nation, but they were few and far between, Haskins says, but they didn't have the capacity to do a large number of mortgages in Black communities. And white banks did not do mortgages to Blacks:

> "In many communities, if you do enough research, you'll find in the deeds still today that there are restrictions where African American Jews and other minorities could not own homes now. Nobody exercises those restrictive covenants, but they still exist."

The 1961 Civil Rights Commission said the financial community acted on the premise that only a homogeneous neighborhood can offer an economically sound investment:

"The Commission on Race and Housing has concluded it is the real estate brokers, builders, and mortgage finance institutions, which translate prejudice into discriminatory action. Thus, at every level of the private housing market members of minority groups meet mutually reinforcing and often unbreakable barriers of rejection."[120]

Black GI's return from World War II to face housing discrimination

More than 1.2 million Black men and women served in the military during World War II, facing segregation, racism and discrimination in the service. The Army, Navy and Marine Corps all segregated Black Americans, often assigning white officers to command them. There were even reports that even German POWs could enter facilities reserved for whites that Black servicemen could not patronize.

But perhaps nothing epitomized the overt racism like the housing discrimination they faced on their return home. That had a huge impact on the cycle of poverty and the racial housing gap that remains both pervasive and illusive.

The GI Bill, officially The Servicemen's Readjustment Act of 1944, was created to help veterans of World War II. It was signed into law by President Franklin Roosevelt who was determined that the returning veterans did not face the same fate as the World War I veterans who marched on Washington during the Great Depression to get "bonus money" that had been promised to them nearly 10 years earlier. The U.S. used army troops to put down that demonstration.

The GI Bill was signed into law to provide low-interest loans for housing, grants for tuition assistance and other types of assistance.

But Southern legislators were successful in pushing administration and implementation of those benefits down to the state level, where racist white administrators did everything that they could to deny those benefits to returning Black veterans.

While the GI Bill's language did not specifically exclude Black veterans from its benefits, it was structured in a way that ultimately shut doors for the 1.2 million Black veterans who had served during the war. Some Southern Democrats feared that returning Black veterans would use public sympathy for veterans to advocate against Jim Crow laws, so they ensured that the bill largely benefited white veterans. They did that by insisting that the benefits be administered by the states rather than the federal government.[121]

That racism in housing was not limited to the GI Bill. Low-cost housing was created to help ease veterans and others in middle class lifestyles. These suburban communities, all called Levittown, were created in New York, Pennsylvania and New Jersey by Abraham Levitt and his sons, William and Alfred. The Veterans Administration and the Federal Housing Administration offered guarantees to builders that qualified veterans could buy homes for a fraction of what they were paying for rent. These homes offered white picket fences, green lawns and modern appliances.

But Black soldiers hoping to live the dream were stopped dead in their tracks. The Levitt's only sold homes to white families, again denying Black families the nation's greatest wealth building asset. These racist rules banning Blacks were written into the covenants of deeds in each the homes built in those communities. By 1953 Levittown had 70,000 residents, but not one of them was Black. (The first Black family did not move in until 1957, and then they experienced attacks on their home and up to 500 whites protesting outside their home.)

And this was not limited to Levittown, according to Haskins:

> "While Levittown got so much coverage, there were so many other communities where...the same thing was occurring."

The Great Recession of 2007-2008

Sometimes referred to as the subprime housing crisis, it occurred after the crash of a U.S. housing bubble and resulted in mortgage foreclosures, delinquencies and a devaluation of mortgage securities. After a dramatic increase in subprime lending, or lower quality mortgages, it ended with a housing crash that resulted in the Great Recession. Millions of Americans lost their homes. Black and Hispanic families were especially hard hit because they were more likely to have a high-cost subprime mortgage.

> "African Americans and other people of color did not recoup as quickly as white people did. We saw the homeownership rate continue to stagnate in these communities, African American community especially," said Rockeymoore.

A generation from now Black family wealth will still be more severely impacted than white family wealth, says a report by the Social Science Research Council and the American Civil Liberties Union.

> "The Great Recession will continue to impact black families more severely in the future in terms of lost potential wealth. By 2031, white wealth is forecast to be 31 percent below what it would have been without the Great Recession, while Black wealth is down almost 40 percent. For a typical black family, median wealth in 2031 will be almost $98,000 lower than it would have been without the Great Recession."[122]

According to Black Star Network's Martin, 8 percent of Black families lost their homes compared to 4.5 percent of white families and 53 percent of Black wealth was wiped out. It will be 100 years to recoup what we lost in 2008.

Racism in home appraisals

More recently Black families have complained of racism in home appraisals. A 2021 study by Freddie Mac found that Black and Latino homeowners are twice as likely as whites to get low home appraisals. The report said 12.5 percent of the properties in predominantly Black census tract areas receive appraisal value lower than contract price vs. 7.4 percent of those is majority white tracts.

"We continue to find that homes in Black neighborhoods are valued at roughly 21 percent to 23 percent below what their valuations would be in non-Black neighborhoods," says a Brookings Institution report. The report "How racial bias affects the devaluation of homes in majority-Black neighborhoods," pegged the cost of those devaluations at across 113 U.S. metro areas in the U.S. $162 billion.

Paul Austin and Tenisha Tate-Austin sued their real estate appraiser after their Marin County, California home was appraised for less than $1 million, or $500,000 less than they expected. As a result, they were denied a loan. When they "white washed" the home (removed all traces of a Black family, including photos and art) a second appraisal came in at $1.4 million. They settled their lawsuit in 2023, but details were not released.

There was a similar case in Baltimore, Maryland. Appraisers valued the home of a university professor and his wife at $472,000. They too "white washed" their home for a second appraisal, which came in at $750,000. There have been similar charges and lawsuits across the country. Only 2 percent of home appraisers are Black, according to a 2018 report from the Appraisal Institute.

Racist lending policies

A *Journal of Financial Economics* study in 2021 found that borrowers from minority groups were charged interest rates that were nearly 8 percent higher and were rejected for loans 14 percent more than those from "privileged groups."

The group, using home loan origination data between 2015 and 2019, found that Black and Latin borrowers paid 4.7 to 4.9 more in basis points for Fannie Mae, Freddie Mac and FHA home purchase loans and 1.5 to 1.6 more for refinancing loans.

Aracely Panameno at the Center for Responsible Lending states:

"From the historical perspective, redlining and discrimination in the financial services shut out the Black community,

"They don't have credit. They can't get credit because they don't have credit, and they don't have credit because they can't get it."

Rep. Mfume, who first entered Congress in 1982, has been active for decades in working to improve Black Americans' fair access to credit, and made important amendments to the Equal Credit Opportunity Law, speaks authoritatively when he says he looked at reports from 33 years ago that showed huge disparities:

"You would think something would have changed. And yet, when you look at these same statistics from last year, you see that nothing has changed."

Philadelphia's Epp emphatically states that the system is rigged.

There are solutions to these housing disparities, most of which require some kind of assistance to increase home ownership in the Black community. They include helping people with down-payment assistance, one of the biggest impediments to home ownership.

Cities across the nation have implemented programs to boost Black home ownership. The mayor of Washington, D.C., for example, has launched a program to increase the number of Black homeowners in the city by 20,000 by 2030.

An important part of that initiative, as with many of the others, involves educating potential homeowners and improving financial literacy. And as important as financial literacy is, by itself it is certainly no panacea for all the ills facing Black America.

Chapter 13: The impact on financial literacy

Financial literacy for the newest Americans was also one of the casualties of the collapse of the Freedman's Bank. That financial knowledge and acumen could have been passed on to future generations and descendants of those former slaves and Black Civil War veterans. Instead, today Blacks lag far behind whites in several measures of financial literacy.

The goal, as Frederick Douglass put it, was to instill in the former slaves "lessons of sobriety, wisdom, and economy, and to show them how to rise in the world."

According to Joseph Haskins of Harbor Bank in Baltimore, "Douglass saw the merits of the bank, which is why he stepped in, recognizing that there needed to be a focus on financial literacy, because it spoke to the economic side of the house". Haskins went on to explain:

> "If there's one area that I think the African American community has come up short on, it is not having given enough emphasis to the economics of life.

> "So, the Freedmen's Bank had many benefits. And it was understood that this institution would not only provide a physical location where someone could bring in deposit, but it would stand as a beacon. It would shine a light on the importance of financial literacy, and the importance of fund management."

In this regard the bank's early success manifested itself in many ways, including financial literacy. In her UCLA PhD dissertation, *"Intergenerational Effects of Wealth Loss: Evidence from the Freedman's Bank,"* Xuanyu (Iris) Fu found that the bank was very successful at promoting schooling and literacy amongst the depositors' children prior to its failure.

Fu found that the bank was able to find education for the depositors' children through its connections with the American Missionary Association (AMA), a Christian educational organization. Many AMA teachers served concurrently as bank cashiers and informed the Black depositors of educational opportunities for their children.

The human capital gains while the bank was in operation were large enough for older children to outweigh and outlast the adverse effect of wealth loss from its failure, she found.

But that success disappeared when the bank disappeared. And the impact has been long-lasting.

Not having the Freedman's Bank to serve as the central place of education *absolutely* had an impact on Blacks financial literacy, thinks Roland Martin.

> "So, we've always had to figure our way out and even and, even when we built our own institutions, we still had to deal with the realities of folks …trying to shut our institutions down through Jim Crow and racism."

That lack of financial education manifests itself in many ways in the Black community, none of them good.

According to the TIAA Institute the financial well-being of Black Americans lags that of the general U.S. population, and whites in particular. The reasons for this gap are complex, but one area of importance in addressing it is increased financial literacy.

Research found that Black Americans exhibit lower financial well-being than the U.S. white population, wrote Annamaria Lusardi, academic director at the Global Financial Literacy Excellence Center.

"Given the strong link between financial literacy and
financial well-being, increased financial knowledge can lead
to improved financial capability and behaviors."

Financial literacy is low among many U.S. adults, especially
African Americans. On average African American adults
answered 38 percent of the P-Fin Index (TIAA Institute-GFLEC)
questions correctly. Only 28 percent answered over one half of
index questions correctly, with 5 percent answering over 75
percent correctly. On average white adults answered 55 percent
of the P-Fin Index questions correctly; 62 percent of whites
answered over half on the index questions correctly and 22
percent answered over 75 percent correctly.[123]

The low financial literacy ratings manifest themselves in many
ways in Black communities across the United States.

- The U.S. Federal Reserve data shows that only 72 percent of
  Blacks have personal credit cards compared to 88 percent of
  whites.
- The majority Black communities have the lowest median
  credit scores and the highest rates of subprime credit scores,
  according to the Urban Institute.
- Non-white Americans are more likely to have more credit card
  debt than emergency savings. 58 percent of Black Americans and
  47 percent of Hispanic Americans say they have more debt than
  savings; just 30 percent of white Americans say the same.
- Majority Black, Hispanic and Native American communities
  have at least 1.5 times the rates of subprime credit scores, debt
  in collections and high-cost non-bank borrowing (such as
  payday loans) compared to majority-white communities,
  according to the Urban Institute.
- Bankrate says a number of factors account for these disparities:
  People of color are most likely to be "credit invisible,"
  meaning they have no credit history; Black communities
  distrust financial institutions; Black communities have less

access to financial services; and racial discrimination is still inherent in the lending process.

"These racial disparities reflect historical inequities that reduced wealth and limited economic choices for communities of color," said the Urban Institute report, *Credit Health During the Covid 19 Pandemic.*

They also have an impact on Black health, according to the National Institute of Health's National Library of Medicine, which found that higher unsecured debt is associated with increased heart attack risk for Black adults, especially among Baby Boomers and during economic recessions.

The NIH report says that studies indicate that debt more often leads to negative consequences for Black than white borrowers. For example:

- Blacks with unpaid medical debt are more likely to lose their homes to foreclosures than whites;
- Black households are disproportionately negatively impacted by the health-consequences of debt from criminal justice fines and fees.
- Blacks with student loans report significantly more debt-related stress than white borrowers, which in turn is linked to increased symptoms of depression and worse self-rated health.

  "Even when controlling for the amount of mortgage debt, Black people experience higher risks of delinquency, foreclosure, and default than Whites," the report says. "It is unknown, however, whether there are racial differences in the relationship between debt and heart attacks."

A growing number of politicians, on both the state and national level, are beginning to see the importance of teaching financial literacy to high school students. And thus, nearly half of the states have some sort of financial literacy requirement for high school graduation. Most require classes, but at least half a dozen also require a standalone financial literacy test before graduation.

That push is being extended to college students as well, prompted by the nation's $1.7 trillion in student loan debt. Black students are more likely than white students to be severely impacted by student loan debt upon graduation. The Brookings Institution estimated that Black students graduate with an average of $52,726 in student debt vs. only $28,006 for white college graduates.[124]

Louis Deas, vice president at Operation Hope, says his organization was founded on the same principles as the Freedman's Bank, promoting financial literacy, particularly for Blacks. Deas explains:

> "We're teaching people about finances, like how to budget … – what the Freedmen's bank would have done."

Both Duke Prof. Darity and Andre Perry, a senior fellow at Brookings Metro, feel strongly, however, that people conveniently use financial literacy to blame people for being in poverty:

> "While teaching high schoolers good financial habits is wonderful, it is absurd to maintain that doing so will close the racial wealth gap," says Perry. "Black people can save every discretionary cent for the next 250 years and it would still not close the racial wealth gap in this country.

> "Increasing financial literary is a noble goal, but a lack of financial literacy did not cause wealth inequalities. If anything, wealthy people need to reckon with how they made their fortunes and who they exploited on the way."[125]

Still, it's clear that the collapse of The Freedman's Bank had a long-lasting impact on the financial literacy of Black Americans. If the bank had survived, it would have meant that bank experience and financial acumen would have been passed down generations, much like it has among middle- and upper-class whites.

The benefits of generations of financial literacy for Black Americans would have been exponential had the bank survived. Key in that knowledge, besides saving, would have been that Blacks would have an enhanced understanding of debt, which has plagued Black Americans for decades. The growing threat of student debt among Blacks has exacerbated the problem.

Chapter 14: Black Americans and debt

Although there has been much emphasis on the racial wealth gap, less attention has been paid to the other side of the household balance sheet: debt.

According to the Aspen Institute debt remains under-appreciated as a driver of the racial wealth gap, especially with the growing problem of student loan debt. [126]

The report says that a post-COVID survey conducted by the Federal Reserve found that millions of households were in a position of net debt rather than net worth, including 10.8 percent of households with zero or negative wealth. Disproportionate numbers of Black households (18.9 percent) were in net debt.

Also, the Aspen Institute says, compared to whites, the debt held by people of color is more likely to be harmful; more likely to involve the court system; and more likely to have spillover non-financial consequences.

The National Library of Medicine report the median debt to asset ratio is 50 percent higher among Blacks than whites.

Student debt

The racial wealth gap also means the student debt burden falls disproportionately on Black students and their families, adding to the racial divide in wealth.

According to the U.S. Department of Education, 86 percent of Black students take out student loan debt compared with around only 68 percent of white students. Black students also typically end up with higher debt than white students, taking out an average of $39,500 in student loans, compared to $29,900 for white students, according to the Legal Defense Fund.

Furthermore, student loan debt can impact wealth beyond just that of the individual student borrower. A 2017 study on parental loans by public health researchers Katrina Walsemann and Jennifer Ailshire found that Black parents are more likely to have child-related student debt than white parents.

The study noted:

> "Black parents and parents with more education, higher income, and higher net worth were more likely to report child-related educational debt than white parents and parents with no degree, low-income, or negative net worth."[127]

Public fines and fees

The protests that followed the police shooting of an unarmed Black man in Ferguson, Missouri resulted in a Justice Department investigation of the city's police department. But more damaging were the investigations that followed the protests.

The Justice Department uncovered a pattern of unfair traffic stops, questionable arrests, unreasonable use of force. A similar pattern was found in the city's court system. A lawsuit found that the city received $2.6 million in court fines and fees, its second largest source of income, from traffic violations and low-level municipal infractions.

The shooting, the Department of Justice found, was part of a broader pattern on the part of the majority-white city council and police, who openly targeted the majority-Black population with fines to raise revenue to address a substantial sales tax shortfall.

It was a pattern of racism in both police and in courts in cities around the U.S. and impacted the wealth and finances of the Black communities.

According to a research report from Michael W. Sances and Hye Young Yu for The London School of Economics:

> "The rise of the Black Lives Matter movement following the 2014 shooting of Michael Brown in Ferguson, Missouri, also focused attention on how police and city officials use fines taken from communities of color to fund city administration,"

In research which examined revenue data from more than 9,000 cities, the authors found that cities with a larger Black population collect a greater number of fines.[128]

Medical debt

Among adults ages 18 to 64, 31 percent of Blacks hold unpaid medical debt compared to just 23 percent of white adults, according to The Annie E. Casey Foundation. Also, in that same age group, nearly a third of Blacks had past-due medical debt compared to 23 percent of white adults.

Mortgage debt

The median mortgage was $130,000 for white borrowers and $116,000 for Black borrowers, according to the Aspen Institute. The amount owed, though, doesn't tell the whole story. Black, Latino, and Native American homeowners have mortgages that are often higher-cost and risker than those made to white borrowers, because they are based on assets, credit history and other factors. While white households borrow more heavily, they also have higher incomes, which means it's easier to pay the larger loans, the Aspen Institute study said.

Black American homeowners, who are much more likely to be offered mortgages with higher interest rates and higher fees, also, typically hold less equity than their white Americans. Among homebuyers, Blacks have the lowest credit scores.

Credit card debt

Black borrowers on average have lower credit scores than white consumers, so their choices are limited, a study by the Urban Institute found.

The average credit card balance for white families was $6,940 in 2021, the most recent figures available that break debt down by race. For Black families, it was $3,940, and for Hispanic families it was $5,510.

But the median debt-to-asset ratio for white families is 26.5 percent, while it was 46.8 percent for Black families, an Employment Benefits Institute study found.

Black Americans have lower credit card debt that whites but pay considerably higher interest on that debt. Also, according to a Bankrate survey, Blacks are more likely to have more credit card debt than emergency savings. Fifty-eight percent of Black Americans say they have more debt than savings, compared to 30 percent of white Americans.

And fewer Blacks have credit cards. Forty percent of Blacks say they don't have a credit card, compared to 21 percent of white Americans.

When you consider that Blacks have median household incomes that are only 60 percent of that of white households, and whites have 10 times the wealth of Black households, the gaps in debt take on a much greater significance, says *The Journal of Blacks in Higher Education.*

> "Whites are able to afford large mortgages, auto loans on luxury vehicles and to carry credit card debt because they have the capability to pay off these debts."

Burial costs

Even in death, there is evidence that Black Americans have been cheated by cynical participants in the funeral industry and the related insurance sector. The case of *O'Keefe v Loewen Group* exposed how local monopolies were created in predominantly poor Black neighborhoods to drive up the costs for those least able to afford it. While the Loewen Group were prosecuted successfully, the case raised questions about practices more broadly in the funeral insurance sector.

All of these problems, especially the lack of banking relationships and debt among Black Americans have had huge negative consequences. Among them: the difficulties Blacks have trying to start and maintain businesses of all types and at all levels.

Chapter 15: The racial wealth gap and the impact on Black business

The long-lasting impact of the failure of the Freedman's Bank extends even to Black businesses trying to grow today.

McKinsey & Company says healthy Black-owned businesses could be a "critical component" in closing the racial wealth gap in the United States. It projects that that wealth gap will cost the country $1 trillion to $1.5 trillion by 2028.

According to McKinsey:

> "Black Americans have never had an equal ability to reap the benefits of business ownership. While about 15 percent of white Americans hold some business equity, only 5 percent of Black Americans do. Among those with business equity, the average Black American's business equity is worth about 50 percent of the average American's and a third of the average white American's." [129]

The Brookings Institution in Washington, D.C., says Black businesses had 1.3 million employees and created 48,549 new jobs in 2020. They added $1.7 billion in payroll to the U.S. economy. But racial disparities have had a huge impact on the growth of Black businesses. Today Black businesses receive less business financing and at higher interest rates that white business.

Also, Black businesses fail at an alarming rate. 8 out of 10 Black businesses failed within the first 18 months of operation. And, a Federal Reserve Bank of New York report in August 2020 found that 58 percent of Black business owners described their business as "at risk." Many are underfunded and unable to get credit from traditional sources, so they depend self-funding and loans from friends and families. They also tend to earn lower revenues in most industries and are overrepresented in low-growth, low-revenue industries such as food service and accommodations, says McKinsey.

> "This gap in business activity contributes to an overall lower level of prosperity for Black families: the median white family's wealth is more than ten times the wealth of the median Black family's wealth. This disparity is also a lost opportunity for the US economy as a whole."

McKinsey says that if existing Black-owned businesses reached the same average revenue as their white-owned industry counterparts, the result would be an additional $200 billion in recurring direct revenues, equal to about $190 billion in additional GDP.[130]

Rep. Mfume, meanwhile, says that the biggest issue for Black businesses has been the lack of access to capital and the lack of access to credit.

> "If you put all these requirements on me that are not put on other people, I lose faith in you and I lose faith in the banking system."

And Black Star CEO Roland Martin adds that of the 2.6 million Black-owned businesses in America, about 2.5 million have one employee. He states that "the problem is any slight shift in the economy can be devastating."

That devastation was evident at the height of the COVID-19 pandemic, when an estimated 40 percent of the nation's Black businesses shut down, many of them for good.

For years, Wall Street itself has also faced accusations of discriminatory practices against African Americans, such as limiting approval for mortgages or not providing enough banking options in minority neighborhoods, which are among the damaging actions identified by Citigroup researchers. Specifically, the study by Citigroup came up with $16 trillion in lost GDP by noting four key racial gaps between African Americans and whites, including $13 trillion lost in potential business revenue because of discriminatory lending to African American entrepreneurs, with an estimated 6.1 million jobs not generated as a result.

On top of the normal challenges of running a business, Black business owners must also navigate a considerable funding gap between white- and Black-owned businesses, wrote Nick Perry in a story for NerdWallet's Fundera.

> "As political movements like Black Lives Matter gain steam across the country, it's important to remember that injustice goes far beyond the justice system. The financial system has also historically discriminated against and oppressed Black business owners."

These statistics show how difficult it is for Black businesses to attain funding. Most find ways to finance the startups on their own.[131]

- 44 percent of Black small business owners start their enterprises using their own money. That compares with 37 percent of all small businesses.
- Owners of Black businesses receive less funding, less often and at higher rates than white businesses. Federal Reserve statistics show that more than 80 percent of white business owners receive at least a percentage of the funding they request from banks, but about 66 percent of business owners of color receive the same levels of fund. When firms owned by people of color receive funding, those loans are about $30,000 less than comparable white-owned businesses and they paid 1.4 percentage points higher rates. According to a report from the Minority Business Development Agency, minority firms paid 7.8 percent on average for loans, compared with 6.4 percent for non-minority firms.

- Nearly 17.5 percent of Black business owners say the primary reason they don't apply for loans is because they believe they will be turned down, compared to 12.7 percent of white business owners.
- The average startup capital for new Black businesses is $35,205 compared to an average of $106,712[10] for white entrepreneurs. That makes a razor-thin margin for failure for Black business owners.
- Black business owners are more likely to rely on friends and family for financial help in the first years of their business. Only 1 percent of Black business owners were able to obtain business loans in their first year of operation compared to 7 percent of white-owned firms. 15 percent of Black business owners receive credit cards, vs. 30 percent of white business owners; 14 percent of Black business owners received personal loans vs. 18 percent of white business owners; and 14 percent of Black business owners received family loans to help finance their startup vs. 9 percent of white businesses.
- Black entrepreneurs also report receiving little to no help from banks in completing complicated loan applications. Only 18 percent of Black business owners said they received assistance from loan officers in completing applications compared to nearly 60 percent of white business owners.

Because of that difficulty receiving financing, many Black businesses are underfinanced and have more difficulty surviving economic shocks, like the Covid-19 pandemic.

Research at the University of California, Santa Cruz, and a report by the National Bureau of Economic Research found that 41 percent of Black-owned businesses—some 440,000 enterprises— were shuttered by COVID-19, compared to just 17 percent of white-owned businesses. The stress of the virus, added to years of systematic racism and economic disparities, has Black businesses still reeling.

"Throughout the business-building process, Black business owners face economic, market, sociocultural, and institutional barriers, which are all linked to racial discrimination in the United States. Economic barriers relate to disempowerment and the costs of low starting levels of capital—for individuals, families, and communities."

Andre Perry, at the Brookings Institution adds:

"If Black businesses and individuals had the same type of cushion as their white counterparts, we would not be in this situation."

Increasing and supporting Black business owners and entrepreneurs would have a dramatic impact on the racial wealth gap.

"The wealth differential between business owners and non-business owners is significant, and this wealth advantage is even more pronounced for minorities and women," said Tiffiany Howard, political science professor at UNLV and Congressional Black Caucus Foundation senior research fellow. The median net worth for Black business owners is 12 times higher than Black non-business owners. While whites have 13 times the wealth of Black Americans, the median wealth gap decreases substantially when comparing the medium wealth of Black and white business owners.[132]

Of course, there are solutions to all these problems. But they will require time, money and dramatic changes public policies. And there are serious questions as to whether any type of enabling legislation can make it through either house of Congress while facing opposition and outright hostility from political conservatives who have made it a point to oppose anything remotely related to diversity and inclusion.

Chapter 16: Reparations, baby bonds and other solutions to the racial wealth gap

The history of racism, discrimination and violence runs deep. Every time Black Americans made progress, it was taken away either legally, such as when the City Council of Manhattan Beach, California used eminent domain in the 1920s to take Bruce's Beach away from a Black couple that operated a resort catering to Black people, or violently, as when the middle-class community in Tulsa and dozens of other Black communities across the country were burned to the ground by white mobs. The result is that Black Americans are far behind white Americans in every economic statistic.

There are tried and true solutions, but they are not likely to be applied to Black America in numbers large enough to solve the issue. And no one of those solutions is likely to solve the problems in itself.

The possible solutions

- The "Baby Bonds" proposal that has been introduced in Congress.
- Housing programs that would reduce the gap between Black and white homeownership – a key component on wealth.
- Guaranteed income programs that have proven to be hugely successful on a smaller scale in a number of U.S. cities and counties.
- And reparations for slavery and Jim Crow, probably the most controversial of them all.

Baby bonds

Baby bonds are universal, publicly-funded child trust accounts. When recipients reach adulthood, they can use the funds for wealth-building activities such as purchasing a home or starting a small business.

Economist Darrick Hamilton at the New School for Social Justice along with William A. Darity of Duke University proposed creating Baby Bonds, which would provide every child, starting at birth, with a significant nest egg for their future.

> "Baby Bonds would enable children of color to begin their adult lives with the economic resources they need to build long-term economic security and generational wealth."

While the U.S. government has enabled the development of many wealth disparities, it similarly possesses the capacity to remedy them, according to Duke University's Samuel Du Bois Center on Social Equity. "One universal, race-conscious policy that can do this is Baby Bonds."

In February 2023, Sen. Booker Corey and Rep. Ayanna Pressley reintroduced the American Opportunity Accounts Act, called the "Baby Bonds Bill." Booker had earlier proposed the legislation, which would create a federally funded savings plan for every child born in the United States.

The accounts would begin with $1,000 with an additional deposit of up to $2,000 each year (depending on the family's income) until the child turns 18. Then he or she gains access to the money to buy a home or pay college tuition.

In its report on Baby Bonds, the Samuel Du Bois Center on Social Equity, says the average Baby Bond account for Black Americans is estimated to be about $29,000 at age 18; the equivalent white Baby Bond account would contain about $15,800.

> "Overall, the proposal would cost approximately $82 billion annually, or less than 10 percent of the annual expenditure on social security."

Morningstar, the financial services giant, in its report found that "baby bonds can have a significant impact on the wealth gap when examining the wealth available to each child when reaching 18," and "supports the concept of baby bonds as a way to help children from lower-income families" as a general principle, but state that any implementation should include analysis of "the effect such programs could have on reducing the racial wealth gap and the trade-offs in program designs."

Their verdict on whether the American Opportunity Accounts Act can address the racial wealth gap was "a resounding, overwhelming yes."[133]

Despite having a dozen co-sponsors in the Senate and nearly as many co-sponsors in the House, the legislation has not advanced. It has virtually no support from Republican legislators.

Meanwhile, several states – New Jersey, Connecticut and Washington, D.C. among them – have proposed baby bond legislation on the state level, though those proposals vary widely on enrollment eligibility and administration.

Guaranteed income

Simply put, guaranteed income is a monthly cash payment to individuals or families that come with no strings attached.

The Shriver Center on Poverty Law in Chicago says a guaranteed income can dramatically reduce poverty and improve families' long-term well-being. "Across the country, pilot programs offering a guaranteed income to local residents have measurably improved participants' financial stability," the organization says.

The idea of guaranteed income is not new. Civil rights leader Martin Luther King Jr. proposed the policy in a speech at Stanford University in 1967:

> "I'm now convinced that the simplest approach will prove to be the most effective – the solution to poverty is to abolish it directly by a now widely discussed measure: the guaranteed income.
>
> "This is something which I believe will go a long, long way toward dealing with the Negro's economic problem and the economic problem which many other poor people confront in our nation."

Stockton, California, started a pilot program in 2019 under former mayor Michael B. Tubbs in which the city gave $500 a month to 125 residents of the city's low-income neighborhoods for two years. After the first year, a study conducted by independent researchers found that full-time employment rose among those who received the guaranteed income and that their financial, physical and emotional health improved.

Mayors for a Guaranteed Income, a group founded by Tubbs in 2020, says pilot programs have been started in a number of cities and counties across the nation.

Similar programs have been initiated in Baltimore, Maryland ($1,000 a month to 200 young parents between 18-24 for two years); Rochester, New York; Harris County, Texas; Anne Arbor, Michigan; Cambridge, Massachusetts; and Los Angeles, California; Houston, Texas; and Chicago, Illinois; and Washington, D.C.

Jeremy Rosen, director of economic justice at the Shriver Center on Poverty Law wrote:

> "Guaranteed income offers the best hope to provide people with resources to make important life choices that everyone

wants the ability to make—where to live, how to invest in a better future through education or starting a business, and how to best support children.

"Where properly targeted, guaranteed income specifically gives this opportunity to people who have been systematically excluded from the financial resources to make these decisions, without imposing a massive administrative burden either to qualify or stay eligible. This is a program everyone should support."

Reparations

While baby bonds plan for the future, and guaranteed income addresses the current income inequality, reparations seek to redress for the historical wrongs endured by Black Americans from 1619 onwards.

"Reparations are for the cumulative intergenerational effects of white supremacy," said William A. Darity, professor of public policy at Duke University.

Consultant and politician Maya Rockeymoore Cummings said:

"People of African heritage were enslaved in this country and prevented from earning wages, off of their own labor. African people basically built the backbone of this country a certainly, made other contributions. And yet, they were prevented by law from actually being rewarded with the wealth of their labor."

There are various groups fighting for reparations for Black Americans. There are those who are seeking reparations for slavery – for ripping millions of people from their homes in African and subjecting them to hundreds of years of servitude to build an American economy based on cotton. Civil rights leader

Malcolm X, in a speech in 1960, called for reparations to "compensate us for the labor stolen from us."
There also need to be changes in how wealth is created and expanded.

The 40 acres and a mule that were promised to the newly freed slaves after the Civil War would have done a lot to help the formerly enslaved towards some level of economic justice. The government had actually started to live up to that promise in a limited way. But in the end, like many other broken promises, this died at the hands of racism and violence.

Meanwhile, 1.5 million white settlers were given 160-acre land grants. The Homestead Act, passed on May 20, 1862, was an attempt to accelerate settlement of the Western territory. It granted adult heads of families 160 acres of surveyed public land. Those granted the property were required to live on and "improve" their plot by cultivating the land, and after five years, the original filer was entitled to the property, free and clear.

Darity and Kristen Mullen in the book *From Here to Equality: Reparations for Black Americans in the Twenty-First Century* say the total amount of reparations should be dictated by the amount necessary to eliminate the wealth disparities between Black and white Americans. That would require an expenditure of $10 to $12 trillion, or $200,000 to $250,000 per eligible recipient annually over 10 years. That would, they say, bring wealth in Black families in line with the wealth of white families.

Darity and Mullen wrote in the introduction:

"Restitution for African Americans would eliminate racial disparities in wealth, income, education, health, sentencing and incarceration, political participation, and subsequent opportunities to engage in American political and social life.

"It will require not only an endeavor to compensate for past repression and exploitation but also an endeavor to offset stubborn existing obstacles to full Black participation in American political and social life."

The U.S. House Judiciary Committee voted HR 40, a reparations bill, out of committee in early 2021. That bill was originally introduced by the late Rep. John Conyers Jr. (D-Mich.) in 1989. There are now nearly 200 House co-sponsors and over 20 Senate co-sponsors for a national reparations law.

Passage remains unlikely, however. The legislation is strongly opposed by Senate Republicans and the majority of white Americans. A nationwide poll from the University of Massachusetts Amherst and WCVB found that 62 percent of respondents opposed reparations to descendants of enslaved people. A Reuters poll found that only 20 percent of the respondents supported reparations.

Reparations are not without precedent either in the U.S. or internationally. Haiti, one of the poorest nations in the world, was forced to pay former French slaveholders reparations for nearly a century after that nation's independence. Some critics blame those reparation payments for the financial and political instability that still plagues Haiti today. Marlene Daut of the University of Virginia called those reparation payments "the greatest heist in history."

In 1862 President Lincoln signed a bill emancipating the enslaved in Washington, D.C. and paid those loyal to the union up to $300 for every enslaved person freed. Tera W. Hunter wrote for the New York Times:

"That's right, slave owners got reparations. Enslaved African Americans got nothing for their generations of stolen bodies, snatched children and expropriated labor other than their mere release from legal bondage."

The British government incurred a huge debt – the largest in history – to pay reparations to slave owners after the abolition of slavery in 1835. The government borrowed £20 million which amounted to 40 percent of the British treasury's income and 5 percent of the GDP.[134]

Naomi Fowler wrote for the Tax Justice Network:

"It's hard to believe but it was only in 2015 that, according to the Treasury, British taxpayers finishing 'paying off' the debt which the British government incurred in order to compensate British slave owners in 1835 because of the abolition of slavery. Not a penny was paid to those who were enslaved and brutalized."[135]

In the U.S., the Japanese American Evacuation Claims Act of 1948 provided compensation to Japanese American who were forcibly removed from the West Coast during World War II for losses of real and personal property. Over $36,974,240 was awarded. In 1988 $20,000 tax-free grants were awarded to eligible Japanese Americans for "the fundamental injustices of evacuation relocation and internment during World War II." More than 80,000 people received those payments.[136]

Reparations in other countries have been done in a variety of ways, said Peter Dixon, a research scientist at Brandeis University who studies reparations. In some instances, when people have been paid, they have received a single check. In other instances, people have received a long-term pension.

In the U.S. more is happening with reparations on the local level. Communities such as Asheville, N.C., and Evanston, Ill., passed reparations bills during the height of the social justice movement during the pandemic. Many other cities and states commissions to study reparations, including San Francisco and Los Angeles California; Kansas City, Missouri; and Boston, Massachusetts.

And 11 U.S. mayors, including the mayors of Los Angeles and Denver, agreed to pay reparations to small groups of Black residents in their cities. The programs would be to compensate for past wrongs, but the mayors did not offer details on how much the programs will cost or how recipients will be chosen.

There has been much activity among U.S. colleges and universities. A report by ABC News says nearly 100 U.S. colleges and universities are studying their ties to slavery. Harvard University set up a $100 million endowment for reparations, acknowledging its part in slavery. The money will be used to close the educational, social and economic gaps that are legacies of racism and slavery the university said.

Georgetown University acknowledged its part in owning and selling slaves by launching a $400 million annual fund to support the descendants of those enslaved on Jesuit plantations in Maryland. Brown University began studying its ties to slavery in a 2006 report and students later voted to pay reparations to the descendants of enslaved people owned by the university's founders. Those reparations would include preference on college admissions and direct payments.

- Legislators in the state of Virginia passed a law that required five public institutions – the University of Virginia, the College of William and Mary, Longwood University, Virginia Commonwealth University and the Virginia Military Institute – to make reparations through scholarships or community-based economic development and memorial programs starting in 2022.
- Students and community organizers at the University of Chicago demanded $1 billion in "reparations" from the university to the South Side of Chicago, as part of a campaign asking the university to respond to its historical ties to slavery and allegations of gentrification.

More than 100 colleges and universities in the United States, England, Canada, Columbia, Scotland and Ireland have joined Universities Studying Slavery (USS).

Among them is the University of Glasgow, which, after studying how it benefitted financially from the institution of slavery, agreed to a program of restorative justice which includes the creation of a center for the study of slavery and a memorial paying tribute to those who were enslaved.

"These schools are focused on sharing best practices and guiding principles as they engage in truth-telling educational projects focused on human bondage and the legacies of racism in their histories," the collective said.

But some reparations proponents, like Darity, say though these programs are commendable, they should not be called reparations. Reparations, he says are direct payments to people who have been wronged.

Darity points out that states and municipalities do not have the resources singularly or collectively to deal with reparations, even though they "created a framework from slavery to 100 years of segregation, mass incarcerations and police shootings of unarmed Blacks. But we need to treat the federal government as a culpable partner."

Andre Perry and Rashawn Ray, fellows at the Brookings Institution in Washington, D.C., are of a similar opinion. In the Brookings Institution article "Why We Need Reparations for Black America", they wrote:

> "Discrimination occurred at the federal, state, and local level. The federal government owes Black people, but we should not forget that municipalities played a role and should play a role in the correction. It may not be in the form of financial

reparations. But in terms of cutting a check, it is within the federal government's purview because their policies made ways for other entities to discriminate."[137]

Housing assistance

According to the Urban Institute, the Black homeownership rate is 42.3 percent compared to the homeownership rate among whites of 72.2 percent. Left unaddressed, the organization said, the Black homeownership rate will fall even further by 2040.

A group of housing and civil rights leaders last year announced an initiative to significantly increase the nation's Black homeownership rate. The National Community Reinvestment Coalition says increasing Black home ownership to 60 percent would address significant barriers to housing access and wealth creation for the Black Community:

> "The United States must make strides to reverse the decline of Black homeownership that has been the trend for most of the last 20 years and ensure home loss protections for its most vulnerable populations during and post COVID-19 economic disruption. Doing so not only ensures the economic stability of families but continues to also carve a path of wealth protection for low-wealth families."[138]

The group says reaching a goal of 60 percent Black home ownership by 2030 would require 3.3 million new Black homeowners:

> "Widespread reform is needed to change the state of Black homeownership and with it the racial wealth divide that keeps African Americans in a cycle of asset poverty. A bold federal program, such as the proposed 21st Century Homestead Act, that focuses on revitalizing large clusters of abandoned properties in cities with hyper-vacancies, paired with federal jobs programs that combine infusing greater

income and homeownership opportunities targeted at African Americans, is the type of plan that needs to be explored to bridge these historic inequalities."[139]

The Black Home Ownership Collaborative, a coalition of more than 100 organizations, has developed a 7-point plan to increase Black home ownership: home ownership counseling; down payment assistance; housing production; credit and lending; civil and consumer rights; homeownership sustainability, and marketing and outreach.

The group also called for increased funding for housing counseling services, and a targeted down-payment assistance program.

Roger Ferguson, former CEO of TIAA, the giant financial services firm, probably said it best. "None of those things is a silver bullet or a magic wand. And the reason I think there's no silver bullet is it's taken us literally hundreds of years to get to this place, and hopefully I don't think it will take 100 years to fix it, but I think it will take some time to undo three centuries of damage."

Until serious consideration is given to at least some of these alternatives, there is nothing within reach that will seriously tackle the ever-growing racial wealth gap.

Chapter 17: Wringing hope from a sea of hopelessness

"History is not was, it is."

- William Faulkner, American author

That quote is quite powerful. Nothing more aptly describes the plight of Black Americans.

As much as some conservative politicians might want to bury or erase the nation's history of poor race relations and racial discrimination, that history is real and it is responsible for the plight of an entire race of people who still suffer the consequences.

As I've said repeatedly in previous chapters, there is a serious and persistent racial wealth gap in America. Prosperity Now says that between 1983 and 2013 median Black household wealth decreased by 75 percent, to $1,700, and Latino household wealth decreased by 50 percent to $2,000.

In an earlier report the organization said it would take 228 years for the average Black family to reach the level of wealth of white families.

Prosperity Now also says that by the year 2024, Black and Latino households are projected to have 60 to 80 percent less wealth than they had in 1983.

In other words, the economic inequalities are worsening. Clearly, Black America and the entire nation are heading for catastrophic consequences. Prosperity Now says:

"If the racial wealth divide is left unaddressed and is not exacerbated further…median Black household wealth is on a path to zero by 2053."

As we discussed in the last chapter, it will take big initiatives and big dollars from the federal government and big businesses to even begin to narrow that racial wealth gap. The initiatives proposed by some U.S. cities and states will help – a little. But federal and state governments, universities and corporations were all complicit in the racism and discrimination that helped create the racial wealth and pay gaps, therefore, they should bear the brunt of the cost.

And what will it cost? Duke's Prof. Darity estimates $14 trillion in reparations. The Rand Corp. says it would cost $1.5 trillion to cut the wealth gap in half, and $3 trillion to eliminate it.

What's the difference in those numbers. Vanessa Williamson at Brookings says:

> "If Black households held a share of national wealth in proportion to their share of the U.S. population it would amount to $12.68 trillion in household wealth, rather than the actual sum of $2.54 trillion. The total racial wealth gap, therefore, is $10.14 trillion."

Most whites, and even some Blacks, reject the notion of reparations because they say this nation should not still be held responsible for something that happened 400 years ago. But the truth is that the effects of slavery and Jim Crow racism, which lasted into the 1960s, leaves Blacks still on an unlevel playing field with white Americans.

Frankly, it would be irresponsible to discuss the myriad of issues having an impact on the lives of Black American without talking about how we got here. As much as we want to, we cannot ignore or wish away the history of injustice and discrimination.

There is no doubt that the race is still suffering the effects of hundreds of years of slavery. But pile on the violent white backlash against Reconstruction, lynchings, Jim Crow, the killing by police of innocent Black men and women like Breonna Taylor and George Floyd.

In her 2017 book, *The Color of Money,* legal scholar Mehrsa Baradaran wrote about those issues. Writer and scholar Ta-Nehisi Coates praised the book in his review.

> "When the Emancipation Proclamation was signed in 1863, the black community owned less than one percent of the United States' total wealth. More than 150 years later, that number has barely budged.... Mehrsa Baradaran challenges the myth that black communities could ever accumulate wealth in a segregated economy. Instead, housing segregation, racism, and Jim Crow credit policies created an inescapable, but hard-to-detect, economic trap for black communities..."

Almost lost in that history is the story of the Freedman's Savings Bank, created at the same time as the much more well-known Freedman's Bureau.

W.E.B. Du Bois is quoted in an earlier chapter as saying the impact of the failure of the Freedman's Bank was worse than an additional 10 years of slavery.

Powerful words, but probably still an understatement. The U.S. Treasury Department says "most individuals lost every penny they had saved." That was bad enough, but the failure left Black Americans with a deep distrust of banks and other financial institutions that still lingers today. Of course, the history of exclusion and discrimination in the industry has done nothing to lessen that distrust.

From the story "Why A 19th century bank failure still matters" on UChicago News:

"…The bank's records also highlight the devastating effects wrought by financial failure, and provide a window into the country's long history of exclusion and racism—including the persistent racial wealth gap and the lingering suspicion that many Black Americans hold toward financial institutions."

So, is there room for optimism? Maybe, but it's hard to be optimistic. Big solutions will be required. But polls show overwhelming opposition by whites to any kind of reparations. States led by Republican governors and/or attorneys general are spearheading attacks on anything remotely associated with diversity and inclusion.

One thing that could significantly reduce the racial wealth gap would be to build on scaling Black businesses with capacity to grow their revenue. In other words, boost the "missing middle" of Black businesses to the next level – those with multiple employees, are in growth industries and have more than $1 million in annual revenue. That would have a huge impact on Black entrepreneurs, Black communities and the U.S. economy as a whole.

Black entrepreneurs have been anchors in Black communities in cities and towns across America throughout the nation's history. Businesses as diverse as North Carolina Mutual Insurance Company in Durham (founded in 1898), GN Bank in Chicago (founded in 1934) and Urban One (founded in 1980) served Black customers when white businesses wouldn't. They hired Black workers when white businesses wouldn't. They created generational wealth for their families, and their profits stayed in the Black community.

There is an urgent need to develop a strategy to scale Black businesses in growth. To do that we must significantly increase the number of Black businesses with over $1 million in revenue.

Minority-owned businesses are likely to be in a financially precarious situation due to factors such as limited access to credit. Black businesses are less likely to have their financing needs met than white-owned businesses.

These disparities affect even the more successful small businesses. Among businesses with good credit scores, Black-owned firms are half as likely as white-owned firms to receive all of the financing they apply for (24% versus 48%).[140] When they do get loans, they pay higher rates.

The work that will be required for this effort is certainly no small task. The goals are attainable, but only through innovative ideas and a coalition of corporations, local, state and federal government, non-profits. Frederick Douglass captures the spirit of the immense challenges that will have to be overcome.

> "It is not the light we need, but fire; it is not a gentle shower, but thunder. We need the storm, the whirlwind and the earthquake."

The goals are lofty, and the tasks are immense. But the result would have a huge impact on the racial wealth and income gaps, stronger Black businesses and sustainable generational wealth building that has so far eluded Black America.

Rodney A. Brooks

Rodney A. Brooks is a veteran financial journalist and author of the book *"Fixing the Racial Wealth Gap: Racism and Discrimination Put Us Here, But This Is How We Can Save Future Generations."* The book was a winner of the National Association of Black Journalists' (NABJ) Outstanding Book Award in 2022 and made the shortlist for the Society for the Advancing Business Editing and Writing (SABEW) Third Annual Best in Business Book Awards.

The former Deputy Managing Editor/Money at USA TODAY, Brooks writes on retirement, personal finance and racial wealth and health disparities. He is a contributor to National Geographic, and he has written for The Washington Post, USA TODAY, AARP, Forbes and The History Channel.

He was a winner of the 2022 SABEW Best in Business Awards for his story in on the widening racial wealth gap and was a finalist for 2021 Dateline Awards competition by the Washington D.C. Chapter of the Society of Professional Journalists.

He was elected to the National Association of Black Journalists Hall of Fame in 2021. He was named a Senior Fellow at Prosperity Now in 2022.

Born in Baltimore and raised in New Jersey, Brooks received a B.S. degree from Cornell University and an executive certificate in financial planning from Georgetown University.

Notes

[1] *The 1619 Project*, edited by Nikole Hannah-Jones, Caitlin Roper, Ilena Silverman and Jake Silverstein, One World, New York, 2021.

[2] "Black and Latino Households Are on a Path To Owning Zero Wealth," Emanuel Nieves, September 12, 2017, *Prosperity Now*.

[3] *Reconstruction in America, Racial Violence after the Civil War, 1865-1876*, Equal Justice Initiative, Montgomery, Alabama, 2020.

[4] *Reconstruction in America, Racial Violence After the Civil War, 1865-1876*, Equal Justice Initiative, Montgomery, Alabama, 2020.

[5] *Reconstruction in America, Racial Violence After the Civil War, 1865-1876*, Equal Justice Initiative, Montgomery, Alabama, 2020.

[6] *From Here To Equality, Reparations For Black Americans In the Twenty-First Century*, William A. Darity Jr. and A. Kirsten Mullen, The University of North Carolina Press, Chapel Hill, 2020.

[7] "The Freedman's Savings and Trust Company and African American Genealogical Research," By Reginald Washington, *Federal Records and African American History*, Summer 1997, Vol. 29, No. 2.

[8] *The Shaping of Black America*, Lerone Bennett, Jr., Johnson Publishing Company, Inc., Chicago, 1975.

[9] "The Destruction of Black Wall Street: Tulsa's 1921 Riot and the Eradication of Accumulated Wealth," Chris M. Messer, Thomas E. Shriver and Alison E. Adams, *The American Journal of Economics and Sociology*, Oct. 28, 2018.

[10] *Self-Defense*, by Carol Anderson, *The 1619 Project*, edited by Nikole Hannah-Jones, Caitlin Roper, Ilena Silverman and Jake Silverstein, One World, New York, 2021.

[11] *The Souls of Black Folks, Essays and Sketches*, W.E.B. Du Bois, 1903.

[12] "Black Hospitals In The United States," Encyclopedia.com.

[13] The Transatlantic Slave Trade, The Equal Justice Initiative, Montgomery Alabama,

[14] *The 1619 Project*, edited by Nikole Hannah-Jones, Caitlin Roper, Ilena Silverman and Jake Silverstein, One World, New York, 2021.

[15] *The 1619 Landing – Virginia's First Africans Report & FAQs, Hampton, Four Centuries on the Bay*, Hampton History Museum.

[16] *The Shaping of Black America*, Lerone Bennett, Jr., Johnson Publishing Company, Inc., Chicago, 1975.

[17] *The 1619 Project*, edited by Nikole Hannah-Jones, Caitlin Roper, Ilena Silverman and Jake Silverstein, One World, New York, 2021.

[18] Fred Zilian, "Rhode Island Dominates North American Slave Trade in 18th Century," *Small State, Big History*.

[19] "The Nego in American History," The Board of Education, City of New York, *Curriculum Bulletin, 1964-65 series*.

[20] "The Nego in American History," The Board of Education, City of New York, *Curriculum Bulletin, 1964-65 series*.

[21] "Slave Rebellions," The editors of *Encyclopedia Britannica*, Britannica.com, updated Aug. 23, 2023.

[22] Slave Rebellions," The editors of *Encyclopedia Britannica*, Britannica.com, updated Aug. 23, 2023.

[23] *The Shaping of Black America*, Lerone Bennett, Jr., Johnson Publishing Company, Inc., Chicago, 1975.

[24] "How slavery became America's first big business," By P.R. Lockhart, *Vox*, Aug. 16, 2019.

[25] *The Contribution of Enslaved Workers to Output and Growth in the Antebellum United States.* Mark Stelznar and Sven Beckert, Washington Center for Equitable Growth, June 24, 2021.

[26] *Sick from Freedom: African American Illness and Suffering During the Civil War and Reconstruction*, Jim Downs, Oxford University Press, 2012.

[27] "How the end of slavery led to starvation and death for millions of Black Americans," Paul Harris, *The Guardian*, June 16, 2012.

[28] *America In Black and White, One National, Indivisible*, Stephan Thernstrom & Abigail Thernstrom," 1997.

[29] *Slavery and Public History: the tough stuff of American memory*, James Oliver Horton, Lois E. Horton, New Press, New York, 2006.

[30] *African American Almanac, 400 Years of Triumph, Courage and Excellence*, Lean'tin Bracks, Visible Ink Press, 2012.

[31] *African Americans in the U.S. Army, American Revolution, 1775-1783,* United States Army, army.mil.

[32] *The Colored Patriots of the American Revolution,* William Cooper Nell and Harriet Beecher Stowe, 1855, General Books edition, 2010.

[33] *African Americans in the U.S. Army, American Revolution, 1775-1783,* United States Army, army.mil.

[34] "Slavery in America," By *History.com* editors, Nov. 12, 2009.

[35] "The Civil War & Emancipation," PBS.org

[36] "Black Soldiers In The U.S. Military During the Civil War," Educator Resources, The National Archives

[37] African American Soldiers During the Civil War, The Library of Congress,

[38] "Black Soldiers In The U.S. Military During the Civil War," Educator Resources, The National Archives.

[39] 54th Massachusetts Regiment, The National Park Service, updated Feb. 13, 2023

[40] "Military Service and Black Families During the Civil War," Barbara A. Gannon, *Black Perspectives,* African American Intellectual History Society, Jan. 11, 2023.

[41] "Military Service and Black Families During the Civil War," Barbara A. Gannon, *Black Perspectives,* African American Intellectual History Society, Jan. 11, 2023.

[42] *Free Blacks Lived in the North, Right?* Henry Louis Gates Jr., The African Americans: Many Rivers to Cross, PBS.org.

[43] "How the end of slavery led to starvation and death for millions of Black Americans," Paul Harris, *The Guardian,* June 16, 2012.

[44] The Freedmen's Bureau, By *History.com* editors, *History.com,* Jan. 1, 2012 (updated Oct. 3, 3018)

[45] The Nego in American History, The Board of Education, City of New York, *Curriculum Bulletin, 1964-65 series.*

[46] *Freedman, Philanthropy and Fraud, A History of the Freedman's Savings Bank,* Carl R. Osthaus, University of Illinois Press, 1976.

[47] *Freedman, Philanthropy and Fraud, A History of the Freedman's Savings Bank*, Carl R. Osthaus, University of Illinois Press, 1976.

[48] *Freedman, Philanthropy and Fraud, A History of the Freedman's Savings Bank*, Carl R. Osthaus, University of Illinois Press, 1976.

[49] Freedman's Bank, Britannica, The editors of *Encyclopedia Britannica*.

[50] *Freedman, Philanthropy and Fraud, A History of the Freedman's Savings Bank*, Carl R. Osthaus, University of Illinois Press, 1976.

[51] "The Freedman's Savings and Trust Company and African American Genealogical Research," By Reginald Washington, Federal Records and African American History, Summer 1997, Vol. 29, No. 2, *Prologue Magazine.*

[52] "The Freedman's Savings and Trust Company and African American Genealogical Research," By Reginald Washington, Federal Records and African American History, Summer 1997, Vol. 29, No. 2, *Prologue Magazine.*

[53] "Pensions and Retirement Among Black Union Army Veterans," Dora L. Costa, National Library of Medicine, September 2010.

[54] "United States, Freedman's Bank Records, 1865-1874," database with images, FamilySearch (https://familysearch.org/ark:/61903/1:1:NSBH-K88 : 9 March 2018), Washington Hendley, ; citing bank Richmond (Independent City), Virginia, United States, NARA microfilm publication M816 (Washington, D.C.: National Archives and Records Administration, 1970); FHL microfilm 928,591.

[55] *The Shaping of Black America*, Lerone Bennett, Jr., Johnson Publishing Company, Chicago, 1975.

[56] *Freedman, Philanthropy and Fraud, A History of the Freedman's Savings Bank*, Carl R. Osthaus, University of Illinois Press, 1976.

[57] *Freedman, Philanthropy and Fraud, A History of the Freedman's Savings Bank*, Carl R. Osthaus, University of Illinois Press, 1976.

[58] *Freedman, Philanthropy and Fraud, A History of the Freedman's Savings Bank*, Carl R. Osthaus, University of Illinois Press, 1976.

[59] *Freedman, Philanthropy and Fraud, A History of the Freedman's Savings Bank*, Carl R. Osthaus, University of Illinois Press, 1976.

[60] *"The Freedman's Savings Bank: Good Intentions Were Not Enough; A Noble Experiment Goes Awry,"* U.S. Treasury Department, Office of the Comptroller of the Currency.

[61] "The Freedman's Savings and Trust Company and African American Genealogical Research," By Reginald Washington, Federal Records and African American History, Summer 1997, Vol. 29, No. 2, *Prologue Magazine.*

[62] "Finance, Advertising and Fraud: The Rise and Fall of the Freedman's Savings Bank," Claire Celerier and Purnoor Tak, University of Toronto – Rotman School of Management and London Business School, Feb. 14, 2023.

[63] "The Freedman's Savings and Trust Company and African American Genealogical Research," By Reginald Washington, Federal Records and African American History, Summer 1997, Vol. 29, No. 2, *Prologue Magazine.*

[64] "United States, Freedman's Bank Records, 1865-1874," FamilySearch (https://familysearch.org/ark:/61903/1:1:NSYX-N29 : 9 March 2018), Samuel William Kemp, ; citing bank New York (City), New York, United States, NARA microfilm publication M816 (Washington, D.C.: National Archives and Records Administration, 1970); FHL microfilm 928,585.

[65] Signature records of William Green, No. 2410, Augusta, Georgia, M816, roll 7, RG 101, NA; For the signature records of Clarissa Green, see signature card after account No. 4687, Augusta, Georgia, M816, roll 7, RG 101, NA

[66] 22 million reasons Black Americans don't trust banks(cq)," Marcus Anthony Hunter, Salon, Sept. 18, 2018.

[67] *Freedman, Philanthropy and Fraud, A History of the Freedman's Savings Bank*, Carl R. Osthaus, University of Illinois Press.

[68] *Freedman, Philanthropy and Fraud, A History of the Freedman's Savings Bank*, Carl R. Osthaus, University of Illinois Press.

[69] "Finance, Advertising and Fraud: The Rise and Fall of the Freedman's Savings Bank," Claire Celerier and Purnoor Tak, University of Toronto

– Rotman School of Management and London Business School, Feb. 14, 2023.

[70] *Freedman, Philanthropy and Fraud, A History of the Freedman's Savings Bank*, Carl R. Osthaus, University of Illinois Press, 1976.

[71] "Life of the Freedman's Bank," U.S. Department of Treasury

[72] U.S. Case Files Approved Pension Applications of Widows and Other Dependents of Civil War Veterans, ca. 1871-ca. 1910.

[73] "The Freedman's Savings and Trust Company and African American Genealogical Research," Reginald Washington, Federal Records and African American History, Summer 1997, Vol. 29, No 2.

[74] Signature records of Dilla Warren

[75] "The Freedman's Savings and Trust Company and African American Genealogical Research," Reginald Washington, Federal Records and African American History, Summer 1997, Vol. 29, No 2.

[76] "Finance, Advertising and Fraud: The Rise and Fall of the Freedman's Savings Bank," Claire Celerier and Purnoor Tak, University of Toronto – Rotman School of Management and London Business School, Feb. 14, 2023.

[77] *Freedman, Philanthropy and Fraud, A History of the Freedman's Savings Bank*, Carl R. Osthaus, University of Illinois Press, 1976.

[78] *Freedman, Philanthropy and Fraud, A History of the Freedman's Savings Bank*, Carl R. Osthaus, University of Illinois Press, 1976

[79] "The Financial Panic of 1873," The U.S. Department of Treasury

[80] "The Panic of 1873," American Experience, PBS

[81] "The Freedmans' Savings Bank: Good Intentions Were Not Enough; A Noble Experiment Goes Awry," Office of the Comptroller of the Currency,

[82] "Finance, Advertising and Fraud: The Rise and Fall of the Freedman's Savings Bank," Claire Celerier and Purnoor Tak, University of Toronto – Rotman School of Management and London Business School, Feb. 14, 2023.

---

[83] *From Here To Equality, Reparations For Black Americans In the Twenty-First Century*, William A. Darity Jr. and A. Kirsten Mullen, The University of North Carolina Press, Chapel Hill, North Carolina, 2020.

[84] *Freedman, Philanthropy and Fraud, A History of the Freedman's Savings Bank*, Carl R. Osthaus, University of Illinois Press, 1976

[85] *Freedman, Philanthropy and Fraud, A History of the Freedman's Savings Bank*, Carl R. Osthaus, University of Illinois Press, 1976

[86] "Finance, Advertising and Fraud: The Rise and Fall of the Freedman's Savings Bank," Claire Celerier and Purnoor Tak, University of Toronto – Rotman School of Management and London Business School, Feb. 14, 2023.

[87] "Finance, Advertising and Fraud: The Rise and Fall of the Freedman's Savings Bank," Claire Celerier and Purnoor Tak, University of Toronto – Rotman School of Management and London Business School, Feb. 14, 2023.

[88] "Finance, Advertising and Fraud: The Rise and Fall of the Freedman's Savings Bank," Claire Celerier and Purnoor Tak, University of Toronto – Rotman School of Management and London Business School, Feb. 14, 2023.

[89] "Finance, Advertising and Fraud: The Rise and Fall of the Freedman's Savings Bank," Claire Celerier and Purnoor Tak, University of Toronto – Rotman School of Management and London Business School, Feb. 14, 2023.

[90] *The Souls of Black Folks, Essays and Sketches,* W.E.B. Du Bois, 1903.

[91] "Finance, Advertising and Fraud: The Rise and Fall of the Freedman's Savings Bank," Claire Celerier and Purnoor Tak, University of Toronto – Rotman School of Management and London Business School, Feb. 14, 2023.

[92] "The Freedman's Savings and Trust Company and African American Genealogical Research," Reginald Washington, Federal Records and African American History, Summer 1997, Vol. 29, No 2.

---

[93] "The Freedman's Savings and Trust Company and African American Genealogical Research," Reginald Washington, Federal Records and African American History, Summer 1997, Vol. 29, No 2.

[94] 22 million reasons Black Americans don't trust banks(cq)," Marcus Anthony Hunter, *Salon*, Sept. 18, 2018.

[95] Black and Brown Americans are chronically underbanked and unbanked. Here's Why That Matters," By Daryl Carter, *The Boston Globe*, Updated Sept. 23, 2023.

[96] "What Would It Take To Close America's Black-White Wealth Gap," *The Rand Review*, May 9, 2023.

[97] "In Nearly Every State People Of Color Are Less Likely To Own Homes Compared to White Households," Alexander Hermann, Joint Center for Housing Studies of Harvard University, Feb. 8, 2023.

[98] "The Connection Between Social Security and Black History Month," National Committee to Preserve Social Security and Medicare, Feb. 11, 2022.

[99] A Lifetime Worth of Benefits: How affordable, high-quality child care will benefit Black women's lifetime earnings and retirement security, National Women's Law Center, April 12, 2021.

[100] "Who Owns The Land: Agricultural Land Ownership By Race/Ethnicity," By Jess Gilbert, Spencer D. Wood and Gwen Sharp, *USDA's Rural America*, Winter 2002, Vol. 17, Issue 4.

[101] 22 million reasons black americans don't trust banks(cq)," Marcus Anthony Hunter, *Salon*, Sept. 18, 2018.

[102] "The Basic Facts About Women in Poverty," Fact Sheet, The Center for American Progress, Aug. 3, 2020.

[103] "Black/white differences in the relationship between debt and the risk of heart attack across cohorts," Jennifer Hamil-Luker and Angela M. O'Rand, SSM Population Health, Feb. 25, 2023

[104] Office of Minority Health Resource Center. "Profile: Black/African Americans." Black/African American - The Office of Minority Health, 22 Aug. 2019

[105] "There's a Racial Gap Even in Bereavement," Carly Stern, OZY.com, 2017.

[106] "A Brief History of Black Hospitals in America," By Brian Brown, TeamHealth, Feb. 11, 2022.

[107] "A Brief History of Black Hospitals in America," By Brian Brown, TeamHealth, Feb. 11, 2022.

[108] "Why African Americans Were More Likely To During The 1918 Flu Pandemic," Rodney A. Brooks, *History.com*, ct. 5, 2020.

[109] "Reductions in 2020 U.S. life expectancy due to COVID-19 and the disproportionate impact on the Black and Latino populations," Theresa Andrasfay and Noreen Goldman, *PNAS*, Jan. 14, 2021.

[110] *Homelessness and Black History," National Alliance to End Homelessness,* Feb. 26, 2021.

[111] "Report of the National Advisory Commission on Civil Disorders," or the Kerner Commission, Feb. 29, 1968.

[112] Christian E. Weller, "African Americans Face Systematic Obstacles To Getting Good Jobs," Center for American Progress, Dec. 5, 2019.

[113] "Homelessness and Black History," National Alliance to End Homelessness, Feb. 26, 2021.

[114] "Racial Equity in Banking Starts With Busting The Myths," By Kendra Newsom Reeves, Mindy Hauptman, Caitlin Guzman Hartman, Ryan Curley, Mike Marcus and Brian O'Malley, Boston Consulting Group, Feb. 2, 2021.

[115] "2021 FDIC Survey of Unbanked and Underbanked Households," FDIC, Last updated July 24, 2023.

[116] "Building Trust in the Financial System is Key to Closing the Wealth Gap," Amalie Zinn, Michael Neal, Vanessa G. Perry, *Urban Wire*, The Urban Institute, June 15, 2023.

[117] *The Color of Law: A Forgotten History of How the Government Segregated America*, Richard Rothstein, Liveright Publishing, New York, 2017.

[118] Housing discrimination underpins the staggering wealth gap between blacks and whites," Pedro da Costa, Economic Policy Institute, April 8, 2019.

[119] *1961 United States Commission on Civil Rights Report*, Book 4, Housing.

[120] *1961 United States Commission on Civil Rights Report*, Book 4, Housing.

[121] "How The GI Bill's Promise Was Denied to a Million Black Veterans," Erin Blakemore, *The History Channel*, June 21, 2019.

[122] *Impact of the U.S. Housing Crisis on The Racial Wealth Gap Across Generations*, Sarah Burd-Sharps, Rebecca Rasch, SSRC and ACLU, June 2015.

[123] "Financial Literacy and Wellness Among African Americans," Paul J. Yakoboski, Annamaria Lusardi, Andrea Hasler, Global Financial Literacy Excellence Center,

[124] "Black-White disparity in student loan debt more than triples after graduation," Judith Scott-Clayton and Jung Li, *Economic Studies and Brookings*, Oct. 20, 2016.

[125] "Financial literacy courses won't solve the racial wealth gap," Andre Perry, *The Hechinger Report*, Feb. 26, 2021.

[126] Katherine Lucas McKay, Joanna Smith-Ramani & Tashfia Hasan, "Disparities In Debt: Why Debt is a Driver in the Racial Wealth Gap," *Aspen Institute*, Feb. 7, 2022.

[127] Marisa Wright, "How Student Loan Forgiveness Can Help Close The Racial Wealth Gap And Advance Economic Justice, Legal Defense Fund, April 17, 2023.

[128] "Cities With More African Americans Rely More on Fines for Revenue," Michael Sances and Hye Young You, London School of Economics, May 2, 2018.

[129] "Building supportive ecosystems for Black-owned U.S. businesses," By David Baboolall, Kalemwork Cook, Nick Noel, Shelley Stewart and Nina Yancey, McKinsey & Co., Oct. 29, 2020.

[130] "Building supportive ecosystems for Black-owned U.S. businesses," By David Baboolall, Kalemwork Cook, Nick Noel, Shelley Stewart and Nina Yancey, McKinsey & Co., Oct. 29, 2020.

[131] "20 Black-owned business statistics," Nick Perry, Fundera by Nerd Wallet, Updated Jan 23, 2023.

[132] Study: Black Entrepreneurship in the United States, The University of Nevada, Las Vegas, July 24, 2020.

[133] "Can Baby Bonds Shrink the Racial Wealth Gap," Aron Szapiro, ct. 6, 2020, *Morningstar*.

[134] "Britain's Slave Owner Compensation Loan, reparations and tax havenry," Naomi Fowler, Tax Justice Network, June 9, 2020.

[135] "Britain's Slave Owner Compensation Loan, reparations and tax havenry," Naomi Fowler, Tax Justice Network, June 9, 2020.

[136] "Japanese Claims Act of July 2, 1948, Case Files, The National Archives.

[137] "Why we need reparations for Black Americans," Andre Perry and Rashawn Ray, Brookings, Washington, D.C., April 14, 2020.

[138] "60 percent Black Home Ownership: A Radical Goal for Black Wealth Development," Dedrick Assante-Muhammad, Jamie Buell, Joshua Devine, National Community Redevelopment Coalition (NCRC), March 2, 2021.

[139] "60 percent Black Home Ownership: A Radical Goal for Black Wealth Development," Dedrick Assante-Muhammad, Jamie Buell, Joshua Devine, National Community Redevelopment Coalition (NCRC), March 2, 2021.

[140] Joint Economic Committee Democrats, *Building an economy that embraces and empowers Black entrepreneurship*.